IN THE
MONEY

WORLD POKER TOUR™

IN THE
MONEY

Antonio Esfandiari

with David Apostolico

Collins

An Imprint of HarperCollinsPublishers

WORLD POKER TOUR™: IN THE MONEY. Copyright © 2006 by WPT Enterprises, Inc. All rights reserved. Printed in the United States of America. No part of this book may be used or reproduced in any manner whatsoever without written permission except in the case of brief quotations embodied in critical articles and reviews. For information address HarperCollins Publishers, 10 East 53rd Street, New York, NY 10022.

HarperCollins books may be purchased for educational, business, or sales promotional use. For information please write: Special Markets Department, Harper-Collins Publishers, 10 East 53rd Street, New York, NY 10022.

FIRST EDITION

Designed by Emily Cavett Taff

Bee Royal Face Card Designs © 2005 The United States Playing Company. All rights reserved.

The image on page 84 © Claude Shade
The image on page 108 © Image Masters PD 1 & the 2004 WSOP
The image on page 124 © *Card Player* magazine

Library of Congress Cataloging-in-Publication Data

ISBN-10: 0-06-076305-1
ISBN-13: 978-0-06-076305-3

06   07   08   09   10   DIX/RRD   10   9   8   7   6   5   4   3   2   1

For my grandmother Malak, whom I love
more than anything in the world.

◆ ◆ ◆ ◆

A special thanks to my father, Bijan,
my mother, Elaheh, my brother, Paul,
and Victoria.

Contents

PREFACE

BY STEVE LIPSCOMB

The World Poker Tour has been a series of all-in bets—from everybody. The WPT founders put their livelihoods on the line, the WPT investors and casinos put their precious resources on the line, and the WPT players put their hearts and souls on the line at every WPT event. No one who follows the sport of poker could have missed the remarkable rise of Antonio "the Magician" Esfandiari to the ranks of superstar poker player. I first met Antonio doing card tricks outside the World Series main event—the kind of tricks that boggle the mind—with a huge crowd gathered around him. I remember thinking that there was something about this guy: a flare, a grace, an undeniable charisma—a rock star waiting for a band. I invited him to help us kick off the World Poker

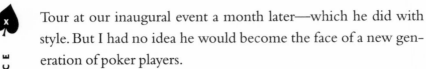

Tour at our inaugural event a month later—which he did with style. But I had no idea he would become the face of a new generation of poker players.

The next time I saw Antonio was when, to his own amazement, he made the final table of our first season World Poker Tour event in San Francisco. At that magic table, the Magician mercilessly tortured Phil Hellmuth, took home an impressive third-place finish, and instantly became a cult hit in the poker world. All this from a guy who had been playing the game seriously for less than a year. He solidified his place in poker history during our second season when he became a World Poker Tour champion and joined the WPT millionaires' club by capturing the prestigious L.A. Poker Classic at the Commerce Casino.

Today, he is one of the most respected and feared players on the tournament circuit—and he continues to serve as a model for the millions of twenty/thirty-something aspiring poker players. In a very short amount of time he has mastered the game, adopted the lifestyle he dreamed of attaining, and managed to remain one of the most gracious and well-liked players in the world. I am not allowed to have favorite players. But, if I were allowed . . . Antonio would be at the top of the list.

What excites me about this book is that players will get a chance to learn from the master how you can get into the game quickly, not get hurt as you get better, and then legitimately have a shot at the big leagues. Only the best magicians dare to share their tricks with the audience—and I think everyone will enjoy and benefit from the revelations.

FOREWORD

BY PHIL LAAK

Antonio Estandiari is one of a kind. I met him at the World Series of Poker in 2000. It was the first time playing there for the both of us. I give Antonio a lot of credit for my current poker career. When I first started playing cards, all I could think about was "Wow, this is fun, I hope I can make enough money that I can justify doing lots of it." However, at that time poker was not nearly as lucrative as it is now. After about a year of playing poker at cardrooms and clubs around the world, I came to the conclusion that it wasn't as lively as I had hoped. I decided to pack my tent, so to say—but more on that later.

After that 2000 World Series of Poker, Antonio and I stayed in touch. At the time, I was living in New York City, my original

Back-to-back WPT champions Antonio Esfandiari and Phil Laak with WPT founder Steve Lipscomb.

stomping grounds for poker back in the day. (I'm sure the true old-timers will get a kick out of me referring to the period 1999–2000 as "back in the day," but considering the current poker landscape, it seems right to me.) Well, it was only a matter of time before a guy like Antonio discovered the Big Apple, and I am honored to have been there for his first adventure.

Antonio came to visit, and I was soon to learn firsthand how much this guy loved spending money. He showed up in New York in the year 2000. Our plan was for one or two nights of cards, some chill time, and hitting the nightlife. Seven nights in all. Sounds simple, right? What I did not know at the time was that the $7,000 he brought with him constituted his entire net worth. He told me it was, and at first I believed him. But I soon figured he was playing me when I saw how this guy spent his money. This guy was full-out sick. Antonio would have sushi delivered for breakfast. The most lavish spots for lunch. A midday massage. And dinner wasn't just dinner. It was an event. We would start with appetizers and drinks, then move on to lobster or steak or whatever was the most extravagant thing on the menu. Then came desserts, coffees, after-dinner drinks—and, of course, if there happened to be any ladies around, we were flipping their bill as well. Before dessert was over, Antonio had scoped out where the hottest place was that night to blow even more money. There was no way $7,000 was all he had. Just no way!

I didn't really notice that we were partying like rock stars until about the third or fourth day when I realized, "Hey, this is a heckuva lot of fun." It was kind of like college, but we spent a lot more money.

At the end of our last night of partying, Antonio looked at me and said "Wow, Phil. I think I spent a lot this week." I echoed, "That's right, sir." The math supported his suspicion. We had spent about $400 a day each. Antonio was down $2,800. I was like "Okay, that was fun, but now it's back to the real world." Antonio, however, had to get right back to the felt when he got home. He had to get unstuck. I didn't understand what the rush was. The poker game wasn't going anywhere.

The rush, of course, was that Antonio had bills to pay. So, of course, a little while later he confirmed that in fact it was all true. He really only had $7,000 to his name. He knowingly and willingly blew 40 percent of his net worth on nothing but making memories. What was he thinking?!? I told him straight up that he was destined for pure ruin if this was part of his normal practice. That night Antonio got a valuable lesson in standard deviation, win rate, and bankroll—all critical concepts to becoming a successful cash-game poker player. He learned how all these things acted in concert and why building your bankroll and not blowing it was so important—at least not until you had your first

$100K squirreled away. Like a sponge, Antonio absorbed everything. "I guess I just need to make a ton of money if I want to keep up this spending," he told me. And that he did.

It wasn't always easy, though. In a nutshell, Antonio was always willing to push it to the next level. He went bust once. How did he respond? He hustled his butt off waiting tables and doing some magic shows to get some money and get right back in action.

But cards were in Antonio's veins, and I think, even back then, that his willingness to dance on the edge would leave him with no other way to go but up. I mean, if you can go all in with 10-6 of diamonds against a known "let's gamble" kind of guy and have it all make sense, and be right, then there really is no other path. He was destined to end up with lots of cash and one sick rep at the tables. I'll get to that 10-6 diamonds hand in a minute.

Long before, and I'm sure long after, the current poker-tournament boom, there were cash games—the bread and butter of poker players. I first discovered poker in 1999 in New York City. I was hooked instantly. As far as hitting the fun quotient, there was no doubt that poker was it. But there is more to life than fun. Money. Money translates to freedom, and freedom is something I am very big on. I was a hungry capitalist, and from what I could see as far as New York poker goes, it wasn't going to meet my financial goals. By the year 2000, I had hopped around from poker club to poker club all over the world, and in the end I just did not see enough money in it to make it worth my while. In hindsight, it is amazing that I once thought that.

Las Vegas happened to be the last of many cities on my poker-research travels and where I first met Antonio. After the 2000 WSOP, I made my final decision. I was calling it quits with poker and going back to Wall Street. I only hoped that I would not have to quit Wall Street for lack of fun.

I was muddling around New York for about six months

when I began getting a call every other day from Antonio. He was telling me of the crazy action back in his hometown of San Jose, California. Huh? Crazy action where? At Bay 101? What is this guy talking about? I had more or less combed the earth looking for the action he spoke of. Well, after like the 10th call that month, I made him swear to me that the numbers he was giving me were not exaggerated. He promised. So I put my Wall Street world on hold and was off to good ole California. The plan was one week in San Jose with five days of poker and two days of chill time.

Wow! It was crazy. In the previous year, I had covered a lot of poker ground: the Vic in London; the Grosvenor in Luton, England; the Concord Card Casino in Vienna; Costa Rica, Atlantic City, Las Vegas, Los Angeles; Colma, near San Francisco; the Aviation in Paris; and countless others. All this in the hopes of finding some sort of poker nirvana. But alas, it did not seem to exist. But now, what was this Bay 101? A wormhole in the poker time-space map, that was for sure. How did I miss this place? I have no idea, but I thank my lucky stars Antonio brought me here.

It was a simple game—Texas Hold 'Em with $10–$20 blinds and a maximum bet allowed of $200. It was called Spread Limit Texas Hold 'Em, a game you never see around anymore. It was Limit Hold 'Em with variable betting. And man, oh man, that place was a gold mine. On the first day, I was told that I broke some sort of record by winning $9,540. Days two through five were up and down, but I had whacked 'em good, and I was hooked. On day seven, I realized that I needed to be near this casino. That was clear. I asked Antonio, "If I left New York tomorrow, would you leave your current living situation and get an apartment with me ten miles or less away from this casino?" That day we signed a lease, and off I went to New York to collect some stuff. And that was that. I was going to California.

If it was not for Antonio, I would probably not have been

pulled back into the world of poker. Thank you, Antonio. The Spread Limit Hold 'Em game eventually died off, and the action seemed to move to Lucky Chances in San Francisco. The new game was No Limit Hold 'Em. Antonio and I had the pleasure of playing poker with some of the finest fish ever pulled from San Francisco Bay. It was a good time. Five years later, Antonio ended up in Las Vegas and I in Los Angeles—two of the biggest poker meccas in the United States. So I thank you, Antonio. For without you, I may never have reemerged into the poker universe.

As anyone who has played the game can attest, there are a lot of ups and downs in poker. You have to be mentally tough to play this game. Just before Antonio's greatest poker success, he suffered through one of his worst periods at the tables. He had built his bank up to about $80,000 when a crazy week of poker began. It was February 2004, and Commerce Casino in Los Angeles was in ultrahigh-buzz mode. The WPT was in town for the L.A. Poker Classic that would begin shortly. Every table was filled, and lots of tables with higher-than-normal stakes were being played. Antonio managed to get a $10–$20 No Limit Hold 'Em game with a $10 ante started. This was a very unusual cash game, and there was some sick gambling going on. In a span of two days, I don't think I have ever seen more bad beats put on one guy than were put on Antonio. He made some huge calls (that were right) and then got sucked out on. And it seems like it was always with this same guy. Antonio must have lost close to 60 grand of his $80K bankroll. The very next day was Day One of the L.A. Classic World Poker Tour event.

But that night was the only time that I ever saw Antonio completely catatonic. He lay on his bed staring at the ceiling completely demoralized like nothing I had ever seen before. You just have to know Antonio. Nothing fazes the guy. That's what makes him a great poker player. You can hit a one-outer and whack him for a ton of money, and he's brushes it off and is on to the next hand. But this night was different. He had outplayed this one guy like a demon, yet this one guy held over Antonio like nothing else and managed to single-handedly cripple his net worth. Antonio was so far gone that I knew the only course of action was to let him be. I never even uttered a single word. "The poor guy," I thought. I think that might be the only time anybody had ever, and will ever, witness him in that state of being. I knew that it was quiet time for Antonio, and I was left wondering when he would resurface for air.

I did not have to wait long. True to his nature, Antonio awoke the next day and had put it all behind him. Like those bad beats had never even happened. I mean, he just lost 75 percent of his net worth outplaying some guy, and one day later it was like a lifetime away and he was on to the World Poker Tour. Well, somewhere in that first hour or two of that tournament, Antonio flopped set over set and the rest was history. It was all over for the rest of us. We were all playing for second place, because first place already had Antonio's name on it. When the tournament came down to the final two players, it was Antonio and Vinny Vinh playing heads-up. They each had about $1 million in chips when Antonio raised preflop with 10-6 of diamonds. Vinny reraised, and Antonio moved all-in. That's right, he moved all-in with 10 high. Vinny thought about it and finally folded. When Antonio turned over his hand, the crowd started yelling, "Vinny's on tilt, Vinny's on tilt." That was the turning point of the tournament. Antonio would go on to win the $1.4 million prize.

I always thought that there was something pure about the juxtaposition of those events. Within a week's time, Antonio experienced a near-all-time low in poker and put it behind him. By doing so, he was able to experience a demon-ripping high.

After this win, you would think Antonio could relax a bit.

He really got over that hump. I mean, with a million or so lying around, it would be tough to blow through that bankroll partying. Well, maybe not. It is Antonio, after all.

Cash games are vastly different from tournament poker. They are the heart and soul of any professional poker player. Cash games are our livelihood. The rising popularity of tournament poker has spawned a whole new generation of poker books. Very few though have dealt exclusively with cash games. And none of them offer the insight and wisdom of the one you have in your hands now. Antonio not only teaches strategy but also offers a lot of advice on developing the right attitude and approach to the game. Whether you are just starting out or a quite an accomplished player, this book is sure to improve your game.

Phil Laak has had great success on the World Poker Tour, winning Season 2's WPT Invitational and making the final table at Season 2's Bicycle Casino's Legends of Poker.

IN THE
MONEY

CHAPTER ONE

My Introduction to Poker

I was nineteen years old sitting in my apartment when I noticed my roommate Scott Stewart running out the door. I asked him where he was going, and he told me he was headed to a poker tournament. What, a poker tournament? "What's a poker tournament?" I asked.

Remember, this was still a few years before the World Poker Tour would bring Texas Hold 'Em into America's living rooms with its revolutionary lipstick-camera coverage. I was soon to be initiated.

I told Scott I wanted to play. He told me before I did that I should read up on the subject. Scott gave me a book to read: *Win-*

ning Low Limit Hold 'Em, by Lee Jones. I read the book in one day and absorbed everything. I was ready to go. The next time Scott went to play a tournament, I went along. There were 120 players entered. I came in first. That's right. I won the very first tournament that I played. To celebrate, I took my girlfriend, Laura, to Hawaii with the winnings.

I was hooked. As excited as I was with my initial success, I knew poker would be hard work. I totally immersed myself into the game of Texas Hold 'Em. I started by playing the low-limit cash games in the cardrooms of northern California. Sometimes the games would move too slow for someone like me, who wanted to learn fast. I wanted to learn as much as I could as quickly as I could.

So I started supplementing my learning curve. There were not a lot of No Limit Hold 'Em games at casinos in those days, so my good friend Gabe Thaler and I started playing heads-up matches at home. Every chance we got, we would play. Neither of us had a big bankroll, but we would play our hearts out. Even though we were good friends, when we sat across from each other we were each playing to win. I wanted his money and he wanted mine. If you do not want it bad enough, you are never going to learn to play the right way.

Gabe and I must have played over a thousand hours of heads-up Texas Hold 'Em. We started out playing $100 no-limit freeze-outs with $1–$2 blinds. We progressed to $200 freeze-outs and then heads-up no-limit cash games with $2–$5 blinds. That is where I first started leaning how to play no-limit poker. I crushed Gabe in those games. More important, though, is that both of our games had improved tremendously. We were each enjoying greater success in the cardrooms. Today, Gabe is one of the best cash-game players I know.

Looking back at that period in my life, I realize how important those heads-up matches were to my development as a poker player. I was able to experience a lot of hands over a short period of time. The game obviously goes much quicker with 2 players as opposed to 10. Playing so many hands provided me with a real sense of hand values and how difficult it is to hit a flop.

Going head to head against a fierce competitor like Gabe helped me immeasurably. I had to fight for every chip. I had to be at the top of my game all of the time in order to win his chips and protect my own. I learned how to study an opponent. Play over a thousand hours with someone and you will know him inside and out. To this day, Gabe is the last person I ever want to face at the poker table, since he knows me so well. That is a critical point. While I came to know Gabe's game very well, he in turn knew my game just as well. Keep that in mind. It is important to know your opponent, but it is equally important to know how your opponent perceives you.

One other thing I should note. If you are going to play, you have to completely divorce yourself from any emotional attachment you may have to your opponent. Gabe was, and is, a very good friend of mine. Yet whenever we sit across the felt from each other, it is every man for himself. Whether you are playing in your home game or the biggest cash games of Las Vegas, you are sure to know some of your opponents. They can look out for themselves. Your job is to look out for yourself.

People often ask me when I decided to be a professional poker player. When I first started out, I totally immersed myself in the game. I was not even thinking about doing this or not doing this for a living. My focus was just on learning as much as I could about the game and playing as much poker as I could. I was still performing magic and working in restaurants to support myself. Poker was a passion. I was willing to play because I believed in my abilities.

Then, one day, Gabe and I found ourselves sitting at home. We were both feeling down because we had each just broken up with our girlfriends. We started talking about how nice it would be to have a $10,000 bankroll. The more we talked, the more we could see it. We had been playing for a while, but it was at that moment that we both knew we were going to be poker players.

A short while later, Gabe and I went to the home of a good friend of ours named Ryan. Ryan is a decent poker player, but he loved to gamble. He just loves action and is one of the sickest gamblers that I know. My entire net worth at the time was only $1,000. I played Ryan heads-up for the entire $1,000 and beat him. We then played for $2,000, and again I won. So I was up to $4,000. I was not as big a gambler as Ryan, so I put $1,000 away, and we played for $3,000. Again I won. He then said, "Let's play for $10,000." I didn't have $10,000. I only had $7,000 to my name. So Ryan said, "I'll tell you what. If you win, I'll pay you within three months, and if I win, you pay me within one year." How could I say no to that? So we played, and I busted him on the second hand. Ryan settled up by paying me $7,000 the next day, giving me $14,000 total. So, all of a sudden, I had my bankroll.

With the phenomenal success of the World Poker Tour, poker tournaments have exploded in popularity over the last few years. Personally, I now play in a lot more tournaments than I did a few years back. Many new players' first introduction to poker has been through tournament play. What these players may not realize, however, is how the strategies involved in cash games vary greatly from those involved in tournament play. In tournaments, you have so many different factors to consider, such as conserving chips, avoiding marginal situations, playing aggressively against short stacks, needing to accumulate chips, and fighting off elimination. In cash games, your decisions are primarily based on how the hand is played and your read of your opponents. This does not mean that the strategies involved in cash games are simpler. The factors that you need to understand in order to evaluate a hand are many and quite complex.

While tournaments are fun and challenging in their own right, cash games are the bread and butter of most poker players. In this book, I offer you the benefit of my experience, which will help you make the right decisions at the poker table and become a winning cash-game player.

Before we get started, let's take a look at how the game is played. Hold 'Em is a seven-card game represented by two cards unique to each player and five community cards that are shared by everyone. Each player then makes his best five-card hand. To begin, each player is dealt two cards facedown. These are the player's *hole* cards, or *down* cards, and can only by seen by the player holding the cards. The cards are dealt clockwise, beginning with the player to the "dealer's" immediate left. The "dealer" is represented by a small white disk called the *button*. With each passing hand, the button is passed to the player to the left. While the casino dealer never changes seats, he deals the cards based on where the button is located.

The first player to the left of the button is called the *small blind*. The second player to the left of the button is called the *big blind*. Together, they are called the blinds. The players in the blinds must post bets before the cards are dealt. The big blind must put in one full bet, and the small blind typically puts in one-half of a full bet. For instance, in a $10–$20 Limit Hold 'Em game, a full bet for the first round is $10. Thus, the big blind must post $10, and the small blind $5. Since the blinds have already posted their bets, after the cards have been dealt, the action begins with the player to the immediate left of the big blind. This player now has the option of calling (matching the full bet amount of the big blind), raising, or folding. In limit play, the player can only raise one full bet, which would be $10 in addition to the original

$10, for $20 total. In no-limit play, the player can raise any amount from $10 to his entire stack.

After the first player acts, the action then continues clockwise around the table. Each player has the option of calling, raising, or folding. In limit play, there is typically a limit to how many total raises there can be in any round of betting. For instance, if there are only four total raises, the action would be capped at $50 (that is, the $10 original bet and four additional $10 raises). In no-limit play, there is no limit to the amount of raises.

When the action gets to the blinds, they have a couple of choices. The small blind is already in for a one-half bet, so if no one has raised, he only has to put in another one-half bet in order to call. Of course, the small blind can raise or fold as well. Depending on what has transpired before the action gets to the big blind, he has a couple of choices. First, if no one has raised the big blind, he can *check,* since he already has posted a full bet. The big blind also has the *option* of raising. Since the big blind had to post his initial bet without the benefit of seeing his cards, he has the option of raising once he has seen his cards.

Once the first round of betting is complete, the dealer will burn one card (the top card on the deck does not play) and then lay three cards faceup in the center of the table. These three cards are turned over simultaneously and colletively are referred to as the *flop.* Everyone at the table can use these community cards. The betting starts anew, with the first player to the left of the dealer who is still in the hand being required to act first. This person can either check or bet. To check means to decline the opportunity to make a bet. You do this either by saying, "Check," or by tapping the table with your hand. If you check, it does not mean you are out of the hand. Do not throw your cards away when you check. Even if you do not like your cards, hold on to them until everyone has had a chance to act. If everyone still in the hand checks as well, then you will get to see the next card for free. That is, you will not have to post any more money. However, once you check, the action will move to the next person going clockwise. That person will now have the same opportunity to check or bet. But as soon as anybody bets, the players who act after the bettor cannot check—they must either fold, call, or raise. Those players who checked before the bettor will also be required to either fold, call, or raise as the action continues around the table. Before we get to the next card, everyone still in the hand must have put in an equal amount of money (the sole exception being when someone is *all-in,* meaning that player has all of his or her chips in the pot).

Once this second round of betting is over, the dealer will now burn another card before turning over one more community card faceup adjacent to the flop cards. This card is called the *turn* card, or *fourth street.* Each player now has six cards from which to make his or her best five-card hand. The betting proceeds exactly as in the second round. In limit play, the betting amounts typically double on this round. For instance, if you are playing $10–$20 Limit Hold 'Em, the betting increments for the first two rounds are $10. In the third and fourth rounds of betting, the betting increments double to $20.

After the third round of betting is complete, the dealer will burn one more card and turn over one last community card. This card is called the *river,* or *fifth street.* Now everyone has seven cards (the five shared community cards and each player's unique two hole cards) from which to make their best five-card hand. Players can use any five-card combination of these seven cards to make a hand. The betting sequence is exactly the same as rounds two and three. Now, after this round of betting is complete, we come to the *showdown.* Each player remaining in the hand will reveal his or her cards, and the best hand will win all of the money in the pot. If, at any point before the showdown, one player makes a bet or raises and no one else calls, then that player wins the pot without a showdown. This can happen in any round of betting from before the flop to fifth street.

Now, let's move on to the next chapters to find out how you can start winning those pots.

CHAPTER TWO

Poker Magic

There I was, before my introduction to poker, going to college like any good kid, and just by walking into a restaurant one day, my life took an unexpected turn. I will never forget that moment. I was sitting at the bar at the Left at Albuquerque restaurant in San Jose, California, and the bartender said to me, "Hey, kid, pick a card."

Whaddya mean, pick a card? The deck was not even open. "Never mind," the bartender said, "just pick a card." I figured everyone picks the ace of spades (maybe that was the trick), so I went with the seven of clubs. The bartender opened up the deck and pulled out a set of playing cards. All 52 cards were there, and

Season 2 WPT Battle of Champions—Phil Laak, David Benyamine, Noli Francisco, Mel Judah, Hoyt Corkins, and Antonio.

51 of them had a blue back. Only one card, the seven of clubs, had a red back. I wanted to do that.

I left the bar and went straight to a magic store and asked the sales clerk to load me up with everything I needed to learn. It took only two months before I dropped out of college and was practicing magic 12 hours a day. I practiced every single day, 12 hours a day, for two years. I went to bed with a deck in my hand. I woke up with a deck in my hand. I went out on dates with a deck in my hand. I even steered my car with my knees and practiced while I drove. That was my life for an entire two years. All I did was practice. My friends got so sick of it. I didn't pay attention to anything else. I was hypnotized. I wanted to be the next David Copperfield. I was performing magic at holiday parties and corporate events and, at the age of 20, was doing rather well for myself.

Of course, magic is an illusion. What looks effortless to the audience is the result of hours and hours of hard work and practice. I was able to become an accomplished magician because I had the discipline to work 12 hours a day every day for over two years. I was able to be so disciplined because I was so passionate about magic.

How do you become a great poker player? I will let you in on a little secret. It is no mystery. There are no hidden formulas. There are no tricks. In short, there is no magic to becoming a successful poker player. Like most anything in life, it takes hard work, patience, practice, and discipline.

Poker is a game of continuous learning. Every time I play, I make sure I learn something new. Whether you are just starting out or have been playing for quite some time, there is always something new to learn. You can learn from playing, observing, reading, or discussing strategy with others. Every player has his own philosophy and perspective. I would like to share mine with you.

BE POSITIVE

Be positive. You will never hear me tell a bad-beat story. Nobody wants to hear it. Think about it. When somebody tells you a bad-beat story, do you care? Besides, everyone who plays the game will suffer his or her fair share of bad beats. That's poker. In fact, the better players will suffer more bad beats than lesser players. That's right. Here's why. If you play well, you will get your opponents staying in hands when you have the better of it, while you will rarely be in that situation. Sometimes, they are going to draw out on you. In the long run, though, you are going to make money in that situation. If you play poker, bad beats are the cost of doing business. Take it in stride and move on. If you dwell on it or let it get to you, it can only have a negative impact on your game.

I have learned to laugh off my bad beats thanks to a little help from my good friend Phil "the Unabomber" Laak. We were playing in a no-limit game in Colma a couple of years ago and I had position on Phil, being seated one seat to his left. Every time he entered a pot, I raised him. If he made it $80, then I made it $300. After a while, he got sick of this, and so he either folded or moved in on me every time that I raised. So after quite a few of these hands, Phil made it $80, and I raised to $300 with pocket jacks. Phil moved all-in for another $5,000, and I thought for a few seconds before I called. There was over $10,000 in the pot. Phil has K-J offsuit, so I was a pretty good favorite here. That did not last long, though. The flop came A-Q-10, giving Phil the nuts with a straight. The turn and the river brought no help, and I lost the hand.

About a month later, we were in Vegas staying at the Bellagio. Phil and another friend, Tony, were up in my room, as we were getting ready to go out for the night. I came out of the shower with a towel wrapped around me and headed toward the dresser to get some clothes. I sensed something was up, as Phil was eyeing me, but I didn't know what it could be. I opened the drawer, and there right on top of my underwear was a J-J across from a K-J with A-Q-10 in the middle. Phil and Tony were laughing hysterically, and I couldn't help but laugh myself.

IN ORDER TO WIN, ONE MUST LOSE

Do not be afraid to lose. Losing is part of winning. Once you accept that, you can get down to the business of winning. You are going to lose sometimes. Accept that and move on. If you go into a tournament or a big cash game afraid of losing, you're done. You will not play right. Fear will show, either in beads of sweat on your forehead or in the slightest hesitation when you are making a monster bet. You will call when you should raise, fold when you should call, limp too often, and then wonder why you never win money. Good players can smell fear a mile away. Show up at the table with the slightest bit of trepidation and the sharks are sure to attack.

YOU CANNOT CARE ABOUT THE MONEY

What's the best way to play fearless? First and foremost, you have to divorce yourself from how you traditionally think of money. Money outside of the poker room is different. That is money to be spent wisely or invested discriminately. The money you bring into the poker room is your means to winning. Do not think of this as money. Think of it as the tools of your trade. You should no more think about the dollar cost of an individual chip than a carpenter thinks about the cost of the nails he's driving. That carpenter will drive all the nails he needs to in order to do the job. That is what I am going to do at the poker table, and that is what you should do as well.

Consider your chips to be the cost of doing business, nothing more and nothing less. As with any business, you will have overhead. Think of bad beats as your overhead. Furthermore, as Doyle Brunson once wrote, when you make a big bet, you cannot think, "Oh man, I'm betting a Cadillac." Even if you're a recreational player, if you're thinking of the steak dinner you could buy with the chips you're betting, you're dead money. So look at those chips as the tools of the trade. You will free yourself from the fear of losing them, and then you can go win more. In order to accomplish this, you should keep a separate poker bankroll. This should be money put aside that you do not need for any other purpose. If you sit down with your rent money, there is no way you are going to be able to play without fear.

Whether you are a professional or a recreational player, only play with money put aside for poker. This should be money you can afford to lose.

CARE NOT WHAT PEOPLE WILL THINK

If you care what people think about your play, you are again playing with fear. Play your game, and everything else will take care of itself. There will be times when you guess wrong and call down a bet when you have the worst of it. There will be times when a bluff attempt fails and you will be forced to turn over losing cards. Concentrate on the process. So long as you make the right decisions at the time, that is all that matters. You will win money in the long run regardless of short-term failures. Make your decisions without fear and without worry of what others think. Table image is critical to success. If you make a failed bluff attempt with confidence, your opponents will think you are wild and dangerous. If you make that same attempt and then blush with embarrassment when called, your opponents will think you are weak.

THE BEST WAY TO MAKE MONEY IS TO FOLD

That's not a misprint. You are reading it correctly: the best way to make money is to fold. If you are playing a full-ring game consisting of 9 or 10 players, you are not going to win every hand. You are not going to come close to winning even half of the hands. You are going to win a small percentage of the total number of hands dealt. You make money by maximizing your profit when you have the better of it and, more important, minimizing your losses when you do not have the better of it. Only play when you have an edge. Unlike in tournaments, you never have to force the action in a cash game. You are never in danger of being blinded out. You can afford to be patient.

This does not mean that you always have to have the best hand in order to take a shot at the pot. You do have to have an edge, though. That edge can be cards, position, table image, or sensing weakness in an opponent. If you do not have an edge, then get out. Casinos make their entire profit by providing games in which the house has an edge. Do not play someone else's edge. Play your own. Poker is a skill, not a gamble. If you want to gamble, go play slots.

Cash games are measured over the long term. Every poker player will have losing sessions and even losing streaks that may last awhile. When you are going through a losing streak, do not let it get to you. Always take time to evaluate your play. If you are making correct decisions, then stay the course.

OBSERVE AND LEARN

As much as I have learned by playing and experimenting, I have also learned a great deal from watching others play. During my thousand-hour heads-up death match with Gabe, I picked up a number of things that helped my game. The guy I have learned the most from is Scott "Scotty" Lundgren, who may be the best cash-game player I have ever seen. Bobby "the Wiz" Hoff taught me how to "build it and take it." That is, you build the pot before the flop and you take it after the flop. Rob Fulop, who worked on the original code for Space Invaders, use to crush the games at Lucky Chances casino, although now he is the guy who never wins. Nonetheless, he taught me a lot. Eldon "Cajun Slick" Elias, Billy O'Connor, and Carl McElvey are other guys who I learned a lot from. I have been fortunate to have had the opportunity to watch and learn from these players, who are all awesome Hold

'Em cash-game players. Even if you do not have access to a Scotty Lundgren, find out who is winning in your cardroom and take the time to study that player. Befriend him and pick his brain. Do everything within your power to keep learning.

When you are not in a hand, do not take time off. Stay in tune with the game. Watch and observe what is going on in front of you instead of eyeing the football game on the television across the room or text messaging your buddy at home. Try to figure out what the other players are holding. You will learn a lot about your opponents this way. Play along with them. This will help enrich your own experience. In a full-ring game, you are only going to play a fraction of the overall hands dealt. So why not learn from all the hands dealt? There is no substitute for experience. If there's 25 hands dealt in an hour at your table, you will be much better off learning from all 25 rather than just the 5 hands you played. Now try multiplying that by the number of hours you play in a session, a week, or even a year. It adds up pretty quickly. Try doing this one session and I guarantee you that you will soon be guessing fairly accurately what cards your opponents are holding.

PRACTICE, PRACTICE, PRACTICE

Like with anything else in life that is worth pursuing, if you want to be good at poker, you need a lot of practice. When I first started pursuing magic, I devoted every free waking moment I had to that pursuit. I had the same dedication to poker because I was just as passionate about it. If I am going to do something, I want to be the best I can be. That's something that is just inbred in my personality. Depending on your viewpoint, I guess that is either a character virtue or a character flaw.

When I first started playing poker, I was still waiting tables and performing magic at Birk's restaurant in Santa Clara to support myself. There was this one time that I went to play Hold 'Em at 11:00 a.m. on a Thursday, and I played until it was time to go to work at 5:00 p.m. When my shift was over, I went straight back to the casino at 11:00 p.m. I played until 10:30 a.m. the following morning before going back to the restaurant for the lunch shift. As soon as the lunch shift was over, I went straight back to the cardroom. By midnight, I started feeling delirious, and the guy next to me said, "You don't look so good." I asked him if it is bad to stay up for a few days without sleep. He replied that it was very bad and that I could do some real damage to my body. Upon hearing that in my already delirious state of mind, I just freaked out. I picked up my chips and went straight home to bed.

Now, I would never recommend playing superlong hours. If you are feeling tired, it is going to affect your play. Unless the game is ultra juicy, I quit when I get tired. You do not need a big bankroll to practice, nor do you need to live near a cardroom in order to get some games in. When Phil Laak and I were roommates, we would play to see who took out the garbage or did the dishes or vacuumed up. Just come up with anything that has value and you can get down to a decent game.

POSITION IS THE NAME OF THE GAME

Texas Hold 'Em is a game of position. If you get to act after your opponent does, you gain information about his hand before he gets information about your hand. It is such a monster advantage to see what your opponent does before you make up your mind about what you want to do. When you have position, you have to exploit that advantage. You have to control the table. You can loosen up your starting requirements. If you are good at reading your opponent's hand, you can win if you have position on him.

Your read then takes precedence over your cards. If you know he does not have a hand, then use position to beat him. To be a winning cash-game player, you have to maximize every advantage you can. After great cards, having position will be the best advantage you will have at the poker table.

NEVER MISS AN OPPORTUNITY TO LEARN AND TO CHALLENGE YOURSELF

Well before I was known as a poker player, Phil Hellmuth held a party at his house for all of the major poker stars playing in the Shooting Star tournament in San Jose. I was not an invited guest. San Jose is my hometown, though, and Phil called to hire me to perform magic at his house. I agreed on one condition. My fee was $250, but I was interested in something else. I told Phil that I would do it, but he would have to play me double or nothing for my whole fee in a game of heads-up No Limit Hold 'Em. Phil graciously agreed.

The party went well, although I could not wait to play him. I returned to his house at a later date for our heads-up match. It did not last long. On about the fourth hand, I had 5-5 and Phil had A-A. Phil raised before the flop and I called. The flop came Q-2-2, and again Phil bet and I called. The five rolled right off on the turn, and I busted Phil.

From the moment I first started playing, I have always challenged myself to be the best poker player I can be. I will challenge and learn from the best. Because of my ego, I have not always been the best with game selection. However, when I have played in games with better players, I observed and soaked in every detail of their play. The lessons I learned more than outweighed any losses I suffered.

Now, I am not suggesting you go out and try to find a game

with top players. What I am saying is that you should always be aware of the players around you, and if you notice some good play, learn from it. I did most of my learning by watching the best. I wanted to play Phil because it was worth $250 for that experience, and hey, if I won, I would get to tell the world that I beat Phil heads-up! To this day, Phil and I are good friends.

A Word about Bankroll

If you are going to make sure that you do not play out of fear, you are going to need a sizable bankroll for the game you are playing. If I am playing No Limit Hold 'Em, I want to make sure that I have the most money on the table. This accomplishes two things. First, I do not lose out on getting all of a player's chips if I can trap him. Next, I can control the table.

Now, if you are just starting out, I would highly recommend that you make your bankroll away from poker. If you are worried about earning your bankroll at the table, you are going to start to worry about the money you are betting. When you sit down to the table, your chips should be viewed as your tools of the trade and nothing more. Once you start looking at those chips as dinner and rent, you're done.

If you are just starting out playing No Limit Hold 'Em, you may want to buy in for a smaller stack. This will minimize your losses until you get accustomed to the game. You can always build your way up to a big stack or buy in for more if you bust out. By starting with a shorter stack, you make your decision process easier. You are more likely to make a tough call than being forced to lay down a superior hand if you do not have to worry about calling off your entire bankroll. Your ultimate goal should be to sit down with the biggest stack, but do not be in a hurry to get there. Poker takes patience and discipline. It's not smart to sit down with the biggest stack if you do not have the skills to take advantage of it. Without the right skills, all you are doing is risking more of your bankroll than is necessary.

DO NOT GET TOO OVERCONFIDENT

There is a big difference between playing without fear and being cocky. Poker can be a humbling game. To play it right requires a great deal of patience and discipline, and the ability to read others. Even if you are the best player at the table, your opponents are not going to roll over for you. You have to pick the right opportunities to attack. To do that requires that you maintain your focus on everything at the table. The moment you think you can go on autopilot and just run over the table is when you are sure to get a rude awakening.

A few years ago, I was doing extremely well, and I was letting my ego get the best of me. I had been playing a lot at the Commerce in Los Angeles and walked in one day to see this big goofball sitting behind a mountain of chips. I sat down at his table salivating as I watched him splash his big stack around. Well, it did not take long before this "goofball" busted me and sent me to my friend's house with my head spinning. Well, that goofball was Scott Lundgren, who I ended up befriending, and I have learned a ton about poker from watching him play. As I said before, he is one of the best cash-game players that I know.

Never let your ego get the best of you. Remember that making money is your goal, and poker is a lifelong game. The best players know that if they have equity in a game and put in the hours, they will make money. Knowing this allows them to keep their confidence level high at all times. As simple as this concept sounds, very few players are able to implement this.

Like I said before, losing is part of winning. Every player is going to have losing streaks. What separates the ultimate winners from the losers is how well you react to your losing streak. Any donkey can win when he is getting cards. What you do when things are not going your way will make or break you as a player.

It is very difficult to maintain your confidence when you are losing even though you are playing well. When your bankroll is taking a hit, it is easy to fall apart. Recognize what kind of player you are. If you need confidence builders, then take the time to work on that. If you are losing, rather than go on tilt, stop for a moment and build your confidence. Take a break or go down a limit. Get yourself a win and then quit for the day on a winning note. Do whatever it is that makes you feel better about your play. The ultimate goal is to be able to build your confidence up to the point that you will no longer need to take time for confidence builders. Your ego will be kept in check. You will be able to keep emotions out of the game. You will soon realize that if you make the right game selection (pick a game in which you have equity) and put the hours in, you will make money. With your newfound confidence and even emotional keel, you will be able to play through losing streaks.

A few years back, Phil Laak and I were roommates in San Jose. One Sunday night, we were driving back from Reno in a snowstorm. I had the wheel, hit an icy patch, and we ended up doing a full 360-degree turn on the freeway. Phil insisted on driving after that. About 10 minutes later, with Phil now behind the wheel, our car took a 180-degree turn and started sliding headfirst into traffic. Fortunately, we were able to avoid hitting anything. Needless to say, though, the incident scared the be-jeezus out of us.

The rest of the way home we drove no greater than five miles per hour. When we finally made it, all I wanted to do was go inside and chill. Phil, on the other hand, got right back in his car and headed to the Garden City Casino. I relaxed, went to bed, and woke up Monday morning to see no Phil. I gave him a call, and he was still playing $20–$40 Limit Hold 'Em. I ran a bunch of errands that day, stopped to see some friends, and finally went to bed. I woke up Tuesday morning and still no Phil. I called him, and he was still playing. Tuesday came and went and, before I knew it, it was Wednesday. Phil was still playing.

Now, back then there were not nearly the number of no-limit cash games that there are today. Lucky Chances in Colma had a great no-limit game on Wednesday that I was really looking forward to. I called Phil that morning, and he said the limit game was too good in San Jose and he was not going to come up to Colma. I played the no-limit game, and by 7 p.m. it was really good. I called Phil. He was up pretty good in his limit game but said that it was dying down, so he decided to take the 45-minute drive to Colma. He got there, and we played until about midnight, when the game broke up. At that point, I decided to go home. Phil, however, was stuck $700 from the no-limit game and said he couldn't quit while being behind, so he went to play a $15–$30 limit game. Now, keep in mind that the $700 Phil was stuck was nothing compared to the $7,000 that he had won over the previous four days back in San Jose. Yet Phil still did not want to be down from his game in Colma. So at around 8 a.m. on Thursday morning, Phil finally came home and proudly announced that he had won $720 at the limit game in Colma, which provided him with the mental strength to quit the game.

While I would not recommend anyone play this long under any circumstances, I include this story to illustrate that even the best players sometime need little confidence builders.

Poker can be a grind. Pro players are notorious night owls. We often play into the wee hours of the morning. With the ever-growing tournament schedule, our lives can be incredibly hectic. There is now plenty of travel and a steady feast of tournaments that can average up to 16 hours a day. In between, we are trying to play as many cash games as possible. Now throw in endorsements, poker camps, interviews, and trying to keep some semblance of a personal life going, and there is not much time for anything else. It could be very hard to live a healthy lifestyle if you do not maintain discipline.

I really believe that a strong body leads to a strong mind. I make sure to eat a healthy diet even when I am on the road. It's so easy when you're playing poker all day to just eat a cheeseburger and fries at the table. If there is nothing healthy available at the table, then take a break and go find something that's good and good for you.

Exercise regularly. Poker tournaments can be grueling. A five-day tournament requires great stamina. Even if you play one-day tournaments, with the growing number of entries, they can last all night. The last thing you want to do is work hard all day to make the final table and then run out of energy just as you are getting close to the real money. Do whatever it takes to stay motivated and keep in shape. I have a long-standing bet with one of my good buddies, David Wells. We each have to work out hard at least four times a week for 45 minutes a session. If either one of us misses a session, we owe the other $500. Money can be a big motivator.

PLAY WITH A CLEAR HEAD

Playing winning poker requires your complete attention. If you are not up to the task, then do not play. If you are having personal problems, or if there is anything else that is going to distract your play, then you are better off not playing. Wait until your head is clear before you get in the game. Avoid looking at poker as an escape. Look at it as your business and put the focus into it that it deserves.

ALWAYS SPREAD MAXIMUM DISINFORMATION

A fellow named Marcus Ru came up with one of my favorite lines of all time: "Always spread maximum disinformation." Poker is a game of incomplete information. Your goal is to try to get a read on your opponents to complete that information. Your opponent's goal is to get a read on you. You have to play offense and defense. Keep those opponents away by mixing up your play and keeping their available information incomplete.

Phil Laak is the absolute best at spreading disinformation. He truly is a genius at making his opponents think that he has no clue when, in fact, he knows exactly what he is doing. Unfortunately for Phil, I think a lot more people are on to him due to his great success and popularity.

THERE IS NO SPOON

Do you remember the creepy little boy from *The Matrix* saying that there is no spoon? If you haven't seen the movie, he meant that the spoon is an illusion. Don't worry about trying to bend it. Rather, look within yourself to make changes. Poker requires a lot of self-reflection. It's impossible to play a perfect game of poker. You can, however, minimize your mistakes and maximize your profits by making correct decisions. Look within yourself to make those decisions and stop worrying about trying to change external forces. If you find yourself constantly begging for the perfect card to peel off the deck, you are looking in the wrong place. Instead, think about how that card can or cannot help you and what you can do with the situation. And, if you haven't seen *The Matrix,* rent it. It's a great movie, and it just may improve your poker game. Remember, there really is no spoon.

MOTIVATION

In order to maintain your focus and maximize every opportunity, you must be properly motivated at the poker table. Cash games can be a grind. The difference between winning players and losing players is a slim one. Often one pot an hour is the difference between the two. Saving a bet or two along the way and picking up a pot in which you don't have anything, but you know your opponent doesn't, either, can make a big difference. If you find yourself just going through the motions, you are not going to do the things that make a difference. Find whatever you can to fuel your motivation.

I started playing poker not long after I graduated from high school. I was considered somewhat of a dork in high school, but that was okay. I used that as a positive force. I wanted to be the guy. I knew I was going to do great things with my life but I just did not know what direction I was headed. After high school, my goal was to go to college and then eventually open up a restaurant and bar and start building an empire. By a twist of fate, I ended up performing magic and then, a couple of years later, playing poker. When I started playing, I put everything I could into the game. I soaked up everything I could and looked for every advantage I could. I wanted to win and achieve great things. Use whatever it takes to keep you motivated. Even though I have had great success in poker, the vision of attending my next high-school reunion still motivates me.

HAVE FUN

Life is too short, so I try to have fun no matter what I am doing. If you are going to play, do whatever you can to make it fun and interesting. Cash games can be a real grind. There's a reason they only show tournaments on television. Playing the right way can be very tedious. If you lose focus, though, you are done. Do whatever you have to do to stay in tune with the game. Make bets with yourself about an opponent's play. If you have a friend at the table, make some side bets. Above all else, stay interested.

I used to play in a regular game with one of the guys I learned a lot from: Eldon Elias. Eldon has been playing poker for over 30 years. He sells fish on the side, and his nickname is Cajun Slick. He won a critical hand with 5-2 once a long time ago, and from then on that hand has been called Cajun Slick in his circle. Well, one night we were playing, and Eldon said to me, "You need a hand named after you." That night, I won three monster pots with 9-7, so I decided that hand was going to be my hand.

"Good," Eldon said. "What are you going to call it?" I thought for a moment or two about it and then announced that from now on the 9-7 would be known as the "Carpet Ride" in my honor. Eldon looked me up and down and then said, "No, from now on 9-7 will be known as the *Persian* Carpet Ride."

So if you are going to play, have some fun. Phil L. and I have come up with a number of acronyms used to describe opponents and situations that we use to keep things lighthearted. A list of some of the more popular ones we use is included at the back of the book.

I try to enjoy every day to the fullest, and I try to find something positive about any situation, no matter how bad it may be. If you lose your entire bankroll at the table, say this to yourself: "I can still take a warm shower in the morning, and not everyone gets to do that." We all tend to take little things for granted in life. Enjoy it while you can, because it'll be over before you know it.

CHAPTER THREE

Getting Started

I am sure many of you who are reading this are very experienced players looking for an edge. However, for those players who are just getting started or who have played many hours online or in home games but never in a casino, let me put your mind at ease. So long as you pick a game that is right for you, you have absolutely nothing to be nervous about. Employ the principles you learn here and just play your game. If you have any questions, do not hesitate to ask. You will typically find that dealers, floor managers, and even the other players are all very helpful. There is no such thing as a bad question—especially when you are putting money at risk.

The original WPT Bad Boys of Poker: Paul Darden Jr., Phil Laak, David "Devilfish" Ulliott, Antonio, and Gus Hansen.

Most casinos have a sign-in desk at the front of the poker room. The games and limits being offered are usually listed, but again, if you have any questions, just ask. Sign up for your game of choice and you will be placed on the list. If the cardroom is not crowded, you could be seated right away, but in today's environment there is usually a wait—especially during peak hours. You are allowed to sign up for as many different games as you like, upping your odds of being seated faster.

A standard Hold 'Em cash game has either 9 or 10 seats at the table—depending on the casino. The tables will usually be filled to capacity. This game is also sometimes called a *ring game* because there is a full ring of people around the table. However, at off-peak times, you may find some empty seats at the table. Games with less than 7 players are referred to as *shorthanded games*. Shorthanded games are more common at off-peak hours. Also, many online poker sites now offer cash games with a maximum of 6 players. You will have to adjust your play for shorthanded games, which we will discuss in a subsequent chapter. Finally, a heads-up game is played between two people. You will rarely find a heads-up cash game in a casino because it is not cost-effective to use up a table and a dealer on just two players. However, heads-up games are becoming increasingly popular online, and I have included a chapter later on discussing specific strategies.

Once you sign up for a game, stay close by so you can hear your name called when your seat opens. Then put your game face on and get ready to play.

So now you are ready to sit down and play a cash game of Texas Hold 'Em. There are a number of general concepts to consider before you sit down, and some others to keep in mind throughout the game.

The first thing to consider is game selection. What level game should you play? You want to choose a game in which you will have equity. That is, you want to enter a game in which you have a positive expected return on your investment. Learn to look at poker objectively, just like you would any investment. Do this even if you are purely a recreational player. After all, whether you are a seasoned professional or a Monday-night home-game player, the object is to win money. So pick a game in which you are likely to be successful. The quality of competition typically increases significantly at each higher level.

In addition to finding a level of competition that you can beat, choose a game that is suitable to your bankroll. Even if you perceive the competition to be weak at a $15–$30 limit game, you should not sit down to this game if you only have $300. You will not be able to play to the best of your ability with such a small bankroll. One bad beat and your bankroll will be severely crippled. With a small bankroll, you are likely to play too cautiously or, worse, play scared. As I mentioned before, if you play with fear, you're done. You will be the hunted, not the hunter.

So what is the correct amount you should buy in for? Personally, in limit games, I like to buy in for about 50 times the amount of the big blind. I find that there is an advantage in sitting down with a large stack. It helps project a stronger table image to your opponents. There is no magic in this number, however. Everyone has his or her own comfort level. If you are more comfortable buying in for 20 or 30 times the big blind in order to minimize potential losses, then by all means do this. However, if you find yourself buying in for 10 times the big blind, you should probably find a lower-limit game. At 10 times the big blind, you are going to smell of scared money, and the sharks at the table will be salivating.

The analysis is a little different when buying in for a no-limit game. The lower no-limit games (such as $1–$2 and $2–$5 blinds) will typically have a maximum buy-in since you can go all-in at any time. Personally, I like to buy in for the maximum. I find this gives me not only a psychological advantage, but also allows me to maximize my equity in the game. I would not sit down to a game if I did not have an advantage. So I want to have enough chips to be able to maximize the profit I can expect from that advantage.

However, if you are moving up a level or want to take a shot at a new game, you have to be careful. At the bigger games, there is no maximum limit to your buy-in. Any game with $5–$10 blinds and above falls into this category. When I sit down to these games, I want to have the deepest stack at the table. That's me, though. In no-limit play, your entire stack could be in jeopardy in any one hand. So buy in for an amount that you would be comfortable losing. You can always buy in for more if you lose your initial amount. It does not do you any good to buy in for a high amount if it is going to cause you to play scared. If you are worried about losing this larger amount, you cannot win. So buy in for the amount that will allow you to play aggressively and not scared.

Again, if you buy in for too small an amount, however, you are giving up too much. At a buy-in for 20 times the big blind, any equity you would otherwise have in the game is greatly diminished. You will not get enough value for a good hand. For example, if you flop the nut flush and an inexperienced opponent has a smaller flush, you are both likely to end up with all of your chips in the pot. By having bought in for a small amount, you will not get maximum value for this hand. Now, let's look at the flip side of this hand. What if we have the smaller flush? If you are going to sit down with a big stack, you have to be able to lay these hands down. That means you have to develop the skill to recognize when your opponent can beat your strong hand and the discipline to let go. If you are not there yet, then do not buy in for a deep stack.

In a no-limit game, there should be a direct correlation to your level of experience and the amount of your buy-in. The more experienced you are, the greater the stack with which you should start. The very experienced players are looking to maximize their profit. They want to have a deep stack in order to get full value out of a favorable hand or to have enough chips to force an opponent out when the situation presents itself. In fact, in the bigger no-limit games, there often is no limit on the maximum buy-in. If you are less experienced, you should consider buying in for a smaller stack. When you buy in for a smaller stack, there are fewer decisions to be made. Most of your decisions will be made preflop based on starting hands and position. With a short stack, you are less likely to get involved in a lot of postflop action unless you hit a very favorable flop. In no-limit play, the toughest decisions come when you have a deep stack and your opponents have deep stacks as well. In these situations, the better and more experienced players have the advantage. So if you are less experienced or are testing a new level, try it with a smaller stack. You can gain some valuable experience without risking your bankroll or giving more experienced players opportunities to outplay you. Just make sure you have enough to be aggressive. If you do not, then find a less-expensive table. You do not want to sit down to a $10–$20 no-limit game with $300 when the average stack is over $2,000. Remember that in order to be aggressive, you have to be wagering an amount that is material to your opponent, not you.

The next thing that you should always remember is that cash games are measured over a long period of time. You are going to have winning and losing sessions. Every player does—even the best in the world have their fair share of losing sessions. Success in poker is measured over the long term. Winning players recognize this. Once you recognize this, it will make it much easier to avoid the short-term emotional setbacks. It is human nature to want instant gratification. Poker can often provide that. On the other hand, poker can just as easily hand you a bad beat. If you let the emotions of these moments affect your play, you will lose focus. One simple way to avoid this is to never tell a bad-beat story. This is such an important point that I am going to repeat it for emphasis: *Never ever* tell a bad-beat story. All that does is reinforce losing—and nobody wants to hear it, anyway.

Learn to view poker in the long term. Losing should not affect how you play. There are some people who just cannot quit when they are losing. They insist on trying to get their money back. What they fail to realize is that oftentimes when they are losing, there is a reason for their losing. They may be playing poorly, or they could be overly tired. In any event, because they are losing, they are likely to have a poor table image. If that is the case, then their opponents have an advantage. When these factors are at hand, then it is probably best to take a break or call it a day. A game will still be there later, or even the next day.

On the other hand, there will be times when you are losing when you should not quit. If you are playing well and believe you are better than the other players at the table, then keep playing, even if you are losing, as long as you feel well and are up to the task. Every player will have his share of ups and downs. Anybody can play well while he is winning. The test of a true poker player is how he does when he is losing.

So how can you tell if you should stay in a game when you are losing? If you are tired and making mistakes, then certainly it is time to go. What is more difficult to recognize, though, are those situations in which your opponents have a good read on you and are attacking you. Always keep in mind how others perceive you. Their perception of you may be a lot different than the image you think you are projecting. If your table image is wrecked, then get out. Go home and play another day.

I am a professional poker player. That means I have to look at poker as my business. Even if you don't play for a living, learn to treat it like a business. As with any business, the main objective is to make money. Also, as with any business, you will have expenses. Antes, blinds, playing pot odds, and suffering bad beats are all part of your expenses. So the next time an opponent hits that two-outer on the river to beat you, keep your emotions in check. Forget about it and move on. And don't tell that bad-beat story!

Now that we know your poker game is your own personal enterprise, we want to maximize your profits. When you are winning, some of your opponents have to be losing. By definition, you have a favorable table image. You have equity in the game. You must take advantage of that table image and maximize your profit in the game. If you fail to do this, then even if you win 7 out of 10 sessions, you still may be a loser overall. If you tend to stay in losing sessions hoping to get your money back and leave your winning sessions early while you are up, you will surely lose a lot more money in your losing sessions than you win in your winning sessions.

How do you take advantage of a favorable table image? Be more aggressive. Never let up on the losing players. Attack them while they are feeling beaten. So long as you are winning, do not leave the table unless you are feeling tired or losing focus. When the game is juicy, satisfy your appetite. Most players do the opposite. They do not want to leave the table when losing because they want to win their money back. Yet when they are winning, oftentimes they will get up in the middle of the game in order to leave a winner. Your equity in the game is always greater when you are winning. Your table image has to be more favorable because you are winning and others have to be losing. If you do not maximize your profit during these sessions, then you jeopardize your ability to make money in the long run. So long as you are feeling well and are able to maintain your focus, stay with the game. The only time you should consider leaving is if you are the type of player who still needs confidence builders and want to make sure you leave on a winning note. With experience, you will no longer need those confidence builders.

There is no substitute for experience at the poker table. With tons of playing hours logged into your subconscious, you will be well equipped to recognize situations and read your opponents. However, just putting in time does not give you experience. Maximize your experience by staying focused every minute you are playing. Study your opponents' mannerisms and watch their betting patterns. There is always something going on at the poker table, whether you are involved in the pot or not. So stay focused and pay attention to everything.

You can learn something from every hand. Experience is what will help you make decisions as you go. For instance, say that I am in the big blind with A-8 offsuit in a limit game. Everyone folds to the player on the button, who raises. The small blind folds and I call. After the turn, the board is 4-5-7-8. With top pair and an overcard, I know I am going to call here. So if I know I am going to call, anyway, I want to be the aggressor. I may even force my opponent to lay down a better hand, such as pocket 10s or pocket jacks. My opponent has to be worried that I have a straight because the hands I could be holding in the big blind are quite varied.

How I play specific situations depends greatly on my read of my opponent. Knowing your opponents helps you make correct decisions. Does this opponent always raise from the button whenever everyone folds to him? Or does he only play strong hands no matter what his position? Some opponents will always bet a scary board no matter what. Others will never bet it unless they have made their hand. Still others will mix it up.

Some players play blindly. They play their cards will little thought to their opponents. If you are this type of player, then focus on your opponents when you are not in a hand so you can dedicate all of your attention to studying them. Try to figure out what they are doing and what kinds of adjustments they are making, if any. Once you've done this for a while, then start thinking about how your opponents are eyeing you up. You must be aware of how your opponents perceive you. Poker is about constantly adjusting. If a player has just lost a hand, you must know how he will react and adjust to that and adjust to how he is adjusting to you. Now, multiply that equation by eight, as that is how many opponents you will have to adjust to as they are adjusting to you. Finally, learn to think about how you can manipulate each player and the situation to your benefit and determine the outcome. When you no longer possess that ability, it is time to get up and leave. If I have doubts about my table image during any particular session, I will run a little test. I'll choose a hand to play aggressively and see how many opponents react. If no one is backing off, then I know it is time to quit. If it does work, however, then it's back to full throttle poker.

By staying focused and paying attention to the subtleties in the game, I can manipulate my opponents to achieve the outcome that I want. Once you know your opponents and know what they think of you, the game will really open up for you. That's when taking advantage of position becomes easier. If I know my opponents, I don't care if I have 7-3 or pocket kings: I can win if I have position. Let me offer an example from a recent cash-game hand.

I am on the button when one player limps in from early position. Three players after him limp in as well. Now the action is on me. Before I even look at my cards, I like my position here. I know the early position limper fairly well. As for the other guys, I am not even worried about them. The fact that none of them raised to try to push anyone out tells me all I need to know. They do not have strong hands here. I do still have to worry about the blinds, though. I look at my hand to see the 6-3 of hearts. I raise to isolate the early position limper. As expected, everyone folds but him. Now, I know he is the kind of guy who could be slow-playing a strong hand here. The flop comes A-7-7. My opponent bets. Now, I know if he had a seven, he would check for sure, because I know he likes to slow-play. I also know that if he had an ace, he would check as well. How do I know that? Because I know how he perceives me. If he checks, he knows I would bet anything. So in his mind, he would believe that he could get more value out of checking his ace than betting it. So what is he betting with?

Now, instead of raising, I just call. By smooth-calling, I show strength. There are no flush or straight draws out there. My opponent has to believe I have something here. Sure enough, the turn comes a blank. My opponent now checks. I bet out and he folds. I cannot tell you how often this scenario happens. That is the value of position and the value of just calling behind somebody to take it away on the next street. More important, that is the value of being active in taking advantage of position. Many a passive player would have mucked that hand preflop or gotten rid of it when he missed the flop. Then he would complain about how he's not getting a hand. A proactive player, on the other hand, creates a winning opportunity by manipulating his opponent with favorable position.

Poker is about hard work and discipline. It is about staying focused at all times and paying attention to every small detail. Over time, by doing this consistently, your increased experience will enable you to see each hand as it is happening and react accordingly. You cannot be on cruise control when you are playing. The great players make money on the subtleties of the game. They make small adjustments that their opponents fail to see. By focusing and paying attention, you will pick up on those subtleties.

Learning the fundamentals is essential before you even sit down to the poker table. Once you begin to play, it is critical to work on your hand-reading skills. Once you gain an understanding of your opponent's play, you can outfox him and defeat him at the table. There is no substitute for experience. Because poker is a game of imperfect information, so much is going to depend on what is commonly referred to as *feel*. What feel really means is relying on your collective experience to recognize situations and understand the type of player your opponent is.

You might be able to get by in the lower-limit games by simply playing solid fundamental poker, but once you are up against some tough competition, relying on fundamentals alone will get you crushed. At the higher-limit and no-limit tables, you must be able to read your opponents and outwit them at the table. However, these tools alone will not bring you success.

Poker is all about making correct decisions. No player will make the right decisions all of the time, but winning players will make them much more frequently than losing players. In order to make correct decisions, you need a firm understanding of the fundamentals. This will require you to learn various odds of making a hand. Once you know the odds, making the correct decision is easy. If you find yourself on a drawing hand, compare the odds of drawing out with the price the pot is offering you.

To illustrate this point, let's look at a sample hand. You are playing No Limit Hold 'Em with $5–$10 blinds. You are in late position, holding 7–8 of hearts, and you call a $10 raise. There's five people in the pot, so that's $100 (five players times $20) plus the $5 small blind (who folded), for a total of $105. Now the flop comes Kh-9c-2h, giving you a flush draw. The big blind bets $20, and two players fold and one player calls. That's an extra $40 added to the pot, for a new total of $145.

The price you are being offered to make your straight on the next card is 145 to 20, or 7.25 to 1. You know that the odds of hitting the flush on the next card are 47 to 9, or 5.22 to 1. (There are 47 remaining cards you have not seen, of which 9 are hearts.) So, on the flop, you are getting 7.25 to 1 in a situation where the true odds are 5.22 to 1. Since the odds are in your favor, you call, bringing the total of the pot to $165.

The turn brings the 3d, which is no help. The first player bets $20 again, and the other remaining player folds to you. Should you call or fold? Again, let's do the math. There is now $185 in the pot ($105 preflop, $60 more on the flop, and now $20 bet at you on the turn). It will cost you $20 more to see if the river card is a heart, which would give you a flush and presumably the winning hand. If you know that of the 46 unseen cards remaining there are only 9 hearts, then you are a 46-to-9, or 5.11-to-1, underdog.

Is it correct to call here? Yes. Your $20 investment will earn you $185, not including additional bets you may make on the river if we hit your hand. Your odds are 9.25 to 1 ($185 divided by 20), which is far greater than the 5.11 to 1 odds of making your hand. Now let's look at this same example under different circumstances): instead of making a $20 bet on the turn, your opponent makes a $100 bet (as you are now playing a no-limit game). Now it will cost you $100 to earn $265. You are only getting paid 2.65 to 1 when the odds of making your hand are still 5.11 to 1. Now it does not make sense to call. (The only exception would be if you think you could make a lot of money by betting on the river if you do hit your hand. Keep in mind that in a no-limit game, you may be able to make a lot on the river if you hit your hand, since you are not limited in how much you can bet or raise. You would bet as much as you think your opponent would call. This is where knowing your opponent is so helpful.)

So here is where we get into a fundamental difference between Limit and No Limit Hold 'Em. In limit play, you are limited to how much you can bet in order to protect your hand. By betting more on the turn, your opponent can make it too expensive for you to try to draw to the flush. That is why it is extremely important to know pot odds. You want to calculate if it is worthwhile to call if you are on a drawing hand. Additionally, however, you want to make sure you bet enough to make it expensive for your opponent to try to draw out on you. Winning poker is all about making correct decisions and forcing your opponent into making wrong decisions. When you bet enough so that it is not correct for your opponent to call you, you really do not care if he calls or not. If he folds, then you have won the pot. If he calls, then he is making a poor decision. Even if he happens to draw out on you, over the long run you will make money when opponents pay too much to draw out on you.

There is a simple trick known as the Rule of Four that can give you fairly accurate odds of making a hand after the flop. What you do is multiply the number of outs you have by four to arrive at your approximate percent chance of making your hand if you play it all the way to the river. For example, say you are playing Jd–10d and the flop brings two more diamonds. You know you have a flush draw, but what are the chances that you will actually make a flush if you play it all the way to the river? First, count your outs. There are 13 diamonds, and you know that 4 of them are out (the 2 in your hand along with the 2 on the board). That leaves 9 remaining diamonds, giving you nine outs. Now, following the Rule of Four, multiply 9 by 4, and you get a 36 percent chance (the actual percentage is 35 percent, but the Rule of Four gets you close enough) that you will make your flush by the river.

Be careful with the Rule of Four, however. In limit play, it is much easier to predict how much money it will cost you if you play your hand all the way to the river. In no-limit play, you never know how much money an opponent will bet on the flop or the turn. A common mistake beginning players make in no limit is to get sucked into a hand for more and more money when they are trying to draw out. As you can start to see, there are a lot of differences between Limit and No Limit Hold 'Em. In the next chapter, we will examine more of those differences.

CHAPTER FOUR

No-Limit versus Limit Games

Being a winning poker player is all about making the right decisions. In order to make those right decisions, you must understand the differences between Limit and No Limit Hold 'Em. If you are going to play both, you must know the correct strategies for each. Many players move from Limit to No Limit Hold 'Em and fail to adjust their play, which can have disastrous consequences on their bankroll. While we will go over the specific strategic differences in subsequent chapters, I would like to take the opportunity here to discuss some of the general fundamental differences between no-limit and limit cash games.

Limit Hold 'Em is more of a science. If you have a good un-

Antonio's digital persona in the new World Poker Tour video game.

derstanding of the starting-hand requirements and know your pot odds, you can do well. Know what hands to play from early, middle, or late position. When you have a strong hand, you want to maximize your value while protecting your hand. In other words, you want to play more "by the book." By definition, you are limited by the rules of the game. You can only bet or raise a predetermined amount. Your opponents know the maximum amount each round of betting can cost them. You are not going to be able to trap an opponent for all his chips when you hit a monster hand. On the other hand, you cannot lose all of your chips in a single bet. You will also have the certainty of how much it will potentially cost you to call down a hand. Limit Hold 'Em is more of a grind.

If Limit Hold 'Em is more of a science, then No Limit Hold 'Em is more of an art. The choices available to you are endless. You have more freedom, and you can be more creative. Your opponents can never be sure how much it will cost them to play a hand and must therefore proceed with caution. The flip side is that you also must be careful. Your opponents also are not limited in how much they can bet at any given time. If an opponent has you covered, then your entire stack is at risk. Of course, you have the opportunity to take your opponent's stack as well. Because of this dynamic, no-limit play becomes a real balancing act. Whenever you raise or reraise, you must be prepared for how your opponent may act. An opponent can come back and move all-in on you. That cannot happen in limit. It is much easier to make a raise in limit, knowing it may only cost you one more bet, as opposed to your entire stack if you are reraised.

In limit play, if you have a good hand, you are almost always better off betting out or raising in hopes of isolating an opponent. Only weak players will limp or call on a frequent basis. In No Limit Hold 'Em, it is often advantageous to limp in. For example, say you have a pair of fives in late position. A player in middle position is the first one to enter the pot, and he makes a standard raise. Everyone folds to you. Now, if you are playing limit, it is a good idea to raise here. Your opponent could have a number of different hands—some of which have you beat, and some of which do not. By raising, you force players behind you to fold, and the original raiser can now either fold, call or reraise. Even if your opponent reraises you, it will only cost you one more bet to see the flop. If you hit the flop, great. If you do not hit it, you still may have a chance to win if your opponent misses the flop as well, because you have position. If you believe your opponent was playing a big ace, you can feel confident betting a flop of three low cards. If a couple of scare cards come on the flop, such as A-K-2, and your opponent checks, you may be able to win the pot with a lesser hand. By betting, your opponent may fold a hand such as a pair of 9s or 10s. This is all possible because you were aggressive preflop and have isolated one opponent.

Now let's look at the same situation in No Limit Hold 'Em.

In late position with a pair of fives and one raiser ahead of you, you are usually better off just calling here. You want to see a flop. If you catch a five on the flop, you have a great chance of winning a really big pot. You are more likely to be in a multiway pot, and if anyone else has caught a piece of the flop, you can make some money. If you miss, you can see what your opponent does. If he bets, you can make an easy fold. If he checks, you can see another free card, or you can make a play if you think he missed the flop. However, if you had raised preflop, you would have run the risk of your opponent making a substantial reraise or even pushing all-in on you. In that case you would have had to lay down your hand, and you would have been unable to even see the flop. Now, by just calling, you may have let some players behind you, including the blinds, see the flop. As we just discussed, if you hit the flop, you have more potential opponents to pay you off. However, what if you are worried someone may have caught a flush or a straight draw that can potentially best your set? In no-limit play, you can protect your hand and make it very expensive for that opponent to chase. You cannot do that in limit play, which is why you want to isolate preflop.

There is a lot more finesse in no-limit play. There is a great opportunity to trap players and win big pots. You can limp in to pots more often with the hopes of hitting a monster flop and cashing in big. Drawing hands such as small pairs and suited connectors have more value in no-limit play because of the nature of the game. For example, say you limp in with a pair of threes and the flop comes A-10-3 rainbow. If an opponent has any big ace, he will have a hard time getting away from the hand. If your opponent has A-10, it will be almost impossible for him to get away from the hand, and you stand an excellent chance of winning his entire stack. In limit play, this would be impossible. If an opponent thinks he may be beat, he can just call you all the way down to the river and lose three bets at most. Even if you miss or get only a piece of the flop with a drawing hand, there are plenty of opportunities to outplay your opponents after the flop in No Limit Hold 'Em. Because you are not limited by how much you can bet or raise, you can take advantage of position and situation and outplay opponents who may have been on a draw as well.

In limit play, the idea is to chip away at your opponents when you have a good hand. You want to get the maximum bets in with the best hand. Premium starting hands have more value in limit play. Big aces such as A-Q or A-J play much better in Limit Hold 'Em than in No Limit Hold 'Em. For example, say you raise with A-Q in middle position in Limit Hold 'Em and you get a late-position raiser. It only costs you one more bet to see the flop. Now say you flop an ace and bet out, only to find the late-position player raising you again. If you know this opponent is hyperaggressive and can have just about anything, you can call him down to the river without risking your entire stack. You just cannot afford to do that in no-limit play. A-Q does not have nearly the equity in no limit. If you flop an ace, you are unlikely to win much of a pot if you have the best hand. Conversely, if an opponent has a hand like A-K, you can lose a lot of money.

No matter if you are playing Limit or No Limit Hold 'Em, you still must play by feel. Everything is situational. You must know your opponents. You must know their betting patterns, their tendencies, and how they adjust when things are going well or poorly for them. You must constantly adjust to the situation. To do this requires focus and total concentration. You must pay attention to everything that is going on at the table. In no-limit play, this is magnified greatly. Make a mistake in no-limit play and it can cost you your entire stack. Make a mistake in limit play and it will only cost you a few bets.

If you are just beginning to play No Limit Hold 'Em, you

may want to start out playing small stacks. Doing this accomplishes two things for you. First, it limits your exposure. You can only lose the chips that you have on the table. Next, it makes the decision-making process easier for you. In no-limit play, the size of your stack makes a difference in your strategy. With a short stack, you will put more emphasis on preflop play. You are not trying to trap opponents as much because you are limited in how much you can win with your short stack. Thus, your strategy should shift to pushing strong hands preflop. You want to practice being aggressive. While it may sound paradoxical, it is often easier for inexperienced players to be aggressive with smaller stacks than larger stacks because they are not putting as much at risk. You can experiment more with different situations without jeopardizing your bankroll. Your ultimate goal would be to eventually sit down at the table with a large stack and play aggressively but not stupid.

While you will learn many general and specific principles in this book, remember that nothing is written in stone in poker. However, once you have a solid understanding of the fundamentals, it will be that much easier for you to know when to deviate from those principles and be creative. By paying attention and focusing on your environment, you will be able to adjust quickly to the action at the table.

One of the hardest adjustments a limit player makes when he takes on no-limit action is knowing the correct amount to bet or raise. In limit, the rules dictate exactly how much you can bet or raise. The only decision you have to make is whether you should bet or raise. In no limit, answering the question of whether you should bet or raise is only the first step. Next, you have to determine how much you should bet or raise. Your choices are almost endless. Making the correct choice, however, is what winning poker players do.

How can you make the correct choice? The first thing you should ask yourself is "What am I trying to accomplish with this raise?" If you are trying to isolate an opponent or win the pot right there, you have to make a substantial bet or raise. If you are trying to add more money to the pot, then you might make a smaller bet (although more experienced players will be suspicious here). Whatever you do, however, you must be prepared for an opponent to reraise you big. A common mistake of beginning players is to make a raise without any forethought to the consequences of that raise. For instance, let's look at a no-limit game where the blinds are $10–$20. A few players limp in front of an inexperienced player who is sitting on the button. This player looks down and sees that he has pocket nines. He figures this is a good hand on the button and raises to $40, or exactly twice the size of the big blind, which coincidentally would be the same amount he would have to raise if he were playing Limit Hold 'Em. Now, this raise is not going to chase anybody out except perhaps the small blind. So what purpose does this raise serve? None as far as I can see. Our inexperienced player may have added more money to the pot, but unless he gets a very favorable flop, he is going to be in a lot of trouble with those nines. However, the real problem with this raise is that he may not get to see a flop at all. By raising, he has now given his opponents the opportunity to reraise. If a player who previously entered the pot slow-plays a big pair, he may now take that opportunity and make a big pot-sized reraise. In limit play, you have a safety net in knowing how much an opponent can raise you at any given time. In no-limit play, there is no such safety net. So long as an opponent has you covered, he can put you all-in at any time.

Whenever you want to make a bet or raise in No Limit Hold 'Em, think about what you are trying to accomplish and then bet accordingly. If you want to isolate or chase people out, then make a big bet. Be smart about your bets, though. Do not bet a lot to win a little. Be careful not to give away your hand with your bet. An oversized bet from an inexperienced player can signal a steal attempt. Take into account how big the blinds are, how big the pot is, your position, and how big your opponents' stacks are before deciding on the correct amount. Once you decide on that amount, ask yourself one last question before committing your chips: Are you prepared for a big reraise from one of your opponents?

Finally, I want to talk about the importance of table image at the poker table. A strong table image is critical to your overall success at any poker table. However, at the lower limits there is only so much you can do. You are likely to get called down more frequently, which is why you only want to see strong hands to the river. Even at the lower limits, though, you can use a strong table image to your advantage. If you are getting pot odds to draw to your four flush and you miss on the river, you can go ahead and bet if you think your opponent missed his draw as well. Many weak players will fold, especially if you have the better table image. If you are in a low-limit game where it seems every hand is played at least fourhanded with at least three players seeing the river, then do not get carried away with your table image. Just concentrate on playing solid, fundamental poker and reading your opponents. Do not overthink the situation or get too crazy in your play. You are most likely going to get a couple of callers no matter what, so push the action when you have the better of it and call when you are getting correct odds to do so. Your cards are going to tell you what to do for the most part.

At the higher limits against toughter competition, players are not so eager to throw their money around on runner-runner straight draws. Players will not blindly call any bet to the river, or they will not last long at the higher levels. Knowing your opponent and his playing habits take on added importance. When you enter a pot, you will often find the hands being played heads-up or maybe threeway. With fewer players in the pot, there is a good chance that no one will hit the flop, or at best only get a small piece of it. In these situations, your cards are not nearly as important as reading your opponent and, more important, keep him from reading you. Mix up your play. Think of what your opponent is thinking. Then think ahead of him.

Do not even sit down to a no-limit table if you are not fully prepared for a tough battle. If you show weakness, opposing players will pounce on you. They will bet and raise you at every opportunity. It is much harder to call a big bet in No Limit Hold 'Em than to make a big bet. Be the aggressor in order to earn that strong table image. Be willing to take calculated risks. Do not be reckless with your risks, though. Do not risk a lot to win a little. Use your chips to isolate opponents when necessary. Use your chips defensively if needed. You cannot let other players consistently push you around. There will be times that you will need to send a message by raising or even reraising, even if you think you have the worst of it. You could still win the hand if your opponent is not strong. More important, you will send a clear message to your opponents that you cannot be pushed around, which will pay off for you in future hands. You cannot play effectively if you are constantly under attack. You want your opponents to respect your play. If they are going to raise you, you want them to know that you may raise back.

While solid, fundamental play is still important in no-limit poker, there will be many more opportunities to take advantage of situations when your cards are secondary. Reading your opponents, using position, and knowing when to make big bets and raises will win you pots that you would never have been able to take in low-limit play. It is a lot easier to steal a pot when you are not limited in how big a bet you can make to steal it. Of course, tough, experienced opponents will be attempting to do the same thing to you. This is where the real battles take place. How do you win? Stay focused, observe everything, anticipate your opponent's moves, and stay one step ahead of what your opponent believes you are likely to do.

Let me offer an example from a hand I played at Lucky Chances Casino that really illustrates how this all comes together and what can be accomplished in no limit. I had pocket sixes with the six of hearts. The board at the end of the hand was 4h-5h-Qs-7h-10h. I made a small value bet on the river with the six-high flush and got raised by an extremely careful player. I would not classify my opponent as tight. Rather, he was very solid, careful, and knowledgeable. When he raised me on the river, I knew he could only have one hand. He had the ace of hearts. He would never raise with the kind of hearts here. How did I know that? Because he would have nothing to gain, since he knew I would not call him unless I had the ace.

So now that I knew he has the nut flush, this was an easy fold, right? I had the six of hearts. If I also had either the three or eight of hearts, I would have a straight flush. Here is where knowing your opponent is critical. I knew this guy was capable of laying down some very big hands. I also had to believe that he knew that I knew that he had the nut flush. So I moved my entire stack into the pot. We both had very deep stacks at the time, so this was an expensive bet. It would also be an expensive call on his part. Well, my opponent thought and thought and thought for what seemed like hours but was just a few minutes. He finally folded his hand. He knew I knew that he had the ace of hearts, and he had to give me credit for the straight flush.

The point of this example is not to recommend that you move in any time your opponent has anything less than the nuts.

In fact, I may not make this move against any other opponent in the world. However, there are two important points I want to make. First, if you stay focused and know your opponents, you will have opportunities to make moves. One big win a session from knowing your opponents can make the difference between a winning and a losing player. Next, I never could have made this move in Limit Hold 'Em. You are never going to bluff someone off an ace-high flush with one more bet. That's the power of No Limit Hold 'Em. It is a more difficult, skillful, and artful game than Limit Hold 'Em. Played correctly, it also can be more rewarding.

CHAPTER FIVE

Cash Games versus Tournament Play

Before we dig into specific cash-game strategy, let's take a minute to look at some of the fundamental differences between cash games and tournaments. With the tremendous popularity of the World Poker Tour, many new players are first introduced to Texas Hold 'Em via tournaments. They watch the latest WPT final table on Wednesday night and want to know how they can play that game. While the fundamentals of Texas Hold 'Em are universal, tournament strategy is greatly different from cash-game strategy. So if you are watching the final table of a major tournament, do not walk into your local cardroom and think you are going to beat the cash games by emulating what you saw on television.

Commerce Casino's Tim Gustin, Vince Van Patten, Shana Hiatt, and Mike Sexton toast Antonio after his winning the 2004 L.A. Poker Classic.

The first major difference between cash games and tournaments is that in tournaments you can only lose the amount of your buy-in. In a cash game, you can lose your entire stack. It's a lot easier to be fearless when all you have at risk is your $50 tournament buy-in as opposed to the $1,000 you bring to the cash game. In a tournament, the chips have no value other than as a means to determine where you place. This brings us to the next big difference. In tournaments, you get instant feedback as to your results. You know by the end of the tournament if you made it to the money and how far you advanced. Cash games are measured over the long haul. Success or failure should not be measured in one session or even a few sessions. If you are looking for instant gratification, cash games are not for you.

Next, in tournaments, everyone starts out with the same number of chips. No one can sit down with a larger stack than anyone else. Everyone starts equally. Also, everyone starts at the same time. (Unless you are Phil Hellmuth, who is notorious for showing up late to tournaments.) You are not entering a game in progress. In cash games, it is up to you to decide how much money you want to put on the table. In the great majority of sessions, you will be sitting down to a game that has been playing for quite some time.

In tournament play, you must constantly adjust to the changing blinds and the introduction of antes. Your table can break up, and you can be moved to a new table. The size of your stack in relation to the blinds and the average-sized chip stack will go a long way in determining your strategy. Since you cannot reach into your pocket to buy more chips, you must make do with what you have. If you are busted in a tournament, you are done. In a cash game, you can always buy more chips.

There will be times that you will play much more aggressively in tournament play than you would in a cash game, and times that you will play much more conservatively than you would in a cash game. Finally, in tournaments you should be playing to win, not finish as high as possible. Anyone can play supertight and advance to the middle of the pack before being eliminated. If you want to make money in a tournament, you have to gun for a top finish. Tournament payouts are weighted heavily to the top three spots. That is going to require you to take a lot of chances to get there. In cash games, your only goal is to make money. You are not competing against anyone else. You should not care if someone else is making more money than you. All you care about is whether you are making correct decisions in your play and are maximizing your profit and minimizing your losses depending on the situation.

The final table of a tournament is remarkably different from even the rest of a tournament, let alone a cash game. Keep that in mind when you are watching the World Poker Tour coverage. You can learn a lot from both the play and the analysis. Some of the things you will learn will be universal to all No Limit Hold 'Em games, such as using position and chips to your advantage. However, a lot of what you will see will only be relative to a tournament final table. Let me offer an example of a couple of hands I played at a final table of a World Series of Poker event that were critical to my winning the tournament and that prestigious WSOP gold bracelet.

With six players left, I was the shortest stack and needed to make a move. Even though I was the short stack, I still had enough chips left to hurt the bigger stacks. So I wanted to make a move before the blinds and antes ate away any more of my stack. With pocket deuces, I moved all-in. I was called by a player with pocket eights, and I was a pretty big underdog. To make matters worse, the flop came 9-10-J, giving my opponent an open-end straight draw to go with his bigger pair. I was down to two outs. The turn brought a five, but the river was the most perfect deuce I've ever seen, and I doubled up. In a cash game, moving all-in with a pair of deuces preflop would be idiotic. If we had deep stacks in the cash game, then calling an all-in bet with pocket eights would be worse. Yet, at the final table of a tournament, both of these moves were correct. I had to make a move, and I could do a lot worse than move in with a pocket pair. Unless someone had two high cards or another pocket pair, they were not going to call me. Even if I got called, I was even money against two high cards. I could only be dominated by a bigger pair, which was what happened here. However, during the course of a tournament, there will be times that you will have to survive an all-in or get lucky when you are making a move with a short stack. In a cash game, you should *never* be relying on luck. There is never a reason why you have to make a move. You cannot be eliminated from a cash game. If you are short stacked and do not want to buy in for any more chips, then do not squander those chips. They can be used another day. Unlike a tournament, you can walk away from the table and keep the chips you have remaining. Those chips have real value. I see a lot of players watch their stacks dwindle in a cash game and then once they are short stacked just throw in the rest on a whim. I do not know what they were thinking, but they were not protecting their bankroll. Cash games are measured over the long term, and how you should play does not vary like it does in a tournament.

Let's get back to the World Series of Poker tournament I was playing. The very next hand after I doubled up with deuces, I looked down to see two beautiful red ladies (queens) in my hand. I raised, only to be reraised by Phil Hellmuth. I moved all-in and Phil called. I showed my queens, and Phil turned over two black kings. Uh-oh. I was in trouble. To make matters worse, the flop came three smaller clubs—J-9-7. I was down to one out—the queen of spades. The turn brought the queen of clubs, giving me a set but making Phil a flush. This did open up some more outs for me, though. The queen of spades was still good, or the board could pair. Any jack, nine, or seven would give me a full house. So I had 10 outs. The river brought a nine, and again I doubled up. I would go on to win the tournament.

I would never commit all of my chips preflop with a pair of queens—especially against Phil Hellmuth—in a cash game. That is not a smart play. You are only going to get called by kings or aces. Late in a tournament, though, is a different story. Phil could have reraised me there with a number of hands, and I did not want him seeing a flop with a hand like A-J or K-Q that could out draw me. In a cash game, if I get reraised when I have queens, I am only going to call at best, and I may even fold depending on my read of my opponent. Even in the tournament, if I had a deeper stack, I could have folded the queens.

Double or Nothing?
Are You Kidding?

by Phil Hellmuth Jr.

When I first learned that there was a poker player/magician in the Bay Area, I asked him if he would do a magic show for me. Giving a little business to a fellow poker player seemed like a good idea—I like to take care of my own. So I arranged for this magician fellow, name of Antonio Esfandiari, to come do some magic tricks at a party I threw. For this particular party (or Dom-fest, there being a plentiful supply of Dom Pérignon on hand), I had invited a bunch of professional-poker-player friends who were in town for Bay 101's Shooting Star tournament. That night, Antonio blew us away with his magic skills, and later on he blew us away with his poker skills!

Of course, Antonio insisted on playing me, double or nothing, for his fee. And, of course, I agreed. A free magic show sounded like a fine idea. So about three months later, with his usual flair, Antonio showed up with a camera crew to film our match. Then the magician dealt me two aces and proceeded to bust me. He had two red fives, and after he raised and I reraised, the flop came down K-3-3. I bet out and Antonio called. The turn card was a five, which sealed my fate. Somehow, some way, Antonio had doubled his fee and busted me, on the Discovery Channel! Did I mention the man has some flair?

The next time Antonio and I met was when we faced each other at the final table of the World Poker Tour's Lucky Chance Championship, held in south San Francisco. We had both made it to the final table with four other players, with television coverage. Antonio took it upon himself to play like a caffeinated Stu Ungar that day. He was raising, reraising, and moving all-in seemingly every hand (I was told later that he did in fact raise or reraise 16 of the first 20 pots.)

This tactic always works, of course, when no one calls you, but oftentimes you do get called; and when you do, you're likely to be a huge underdog to win an enormous pot. The classic saying goes "You win every pot till the last one." In any case, Antonio moved over top of me countless times, slowly dechipping me in the process. Yes, it's true that if I had picked up one hand, he may have run himself aground. But perhaps not. Perhaps he was reading me well enough to dodge the big roundhouse that I had waiting for him, the roundhouse that I use so often against the superaggressive players.

I never found out, since I never did pick up a big hand. And as I moved lower and lower in chips, the prospects looked pretty grim for me. Finally, I did win a couple of pots and was right back in it. But then I made a mistake, a mistake that Antonio helped force me to make. After losing every pot to him all day long, I simply moved all-in, in the small blind, with K-J, for $170,000 when the blinds were at $5,000–$10,000. (Normally, I would open for about $35,000 or so, but Antonio kept reraising me, and I wanted to win a pot, any pot, from him.) Antonio was in the big blind, and I give him max credit for the call he made with his K-Q. He busted me out in fourth place, and went on to finish third himself.

Later the next year, I invited Antonio and his pal Phil "the Unabomber" Laak to speak with me at a lecture for the Learning Annex that I was giving in San Francisco. Antonio and Laak agreed to do it for free—the Learning Annex fees are very modest—as long as I joined them at the Top of the Mark nightclub afterward.

"Okay, sounds great," I told them, and I went out and bought a bottle of Dom Pérignon so that we could open it right after the lecture. After downing this tasty bottle, we drove to the Mark Hopkins Hotel and took the VIP elevator to the Top. From our VIP table at the edge of the dance floor, you could see that the place was blowing up! At my urging, we ordered several more bottles of Dom Pérignon, as well as Petrossian caviar with the traditional Russian buckwheat pancakes on the side. Phil L. was not drinking that night, but he kept bringing over beautiful women to enjoy the DP and our company.

After that enjoyable night out (where I had a bit too much to drink), we asked for the bill. I wasn't too surprised to see that it was over $2,000! Antonio,

Phil L., and I decided to play liar's poker for the bill. Fortunately for me, Antonio lost this time, and we were off to his San Francisco apartment, a fine one with a great view of the city.

Phase three of the evening saw me playing No Limit Hold 'Em at Ultimate-Bet.com at 3:00 a.m., while sitting in a near-drunken state on Antonio's couch. Naturally, I yelled out loud when I took a few bad beats (Poker Brat!), and the next thing I knew Antonio had logged on, joining the game from a different room in his apartment. Before the smoke cleared, Antonio, who had lost the battle at liar's poker, won the war, cashing out $6,500 ahead. Meanwhile, I, who had won the battle at liar's poker, lost this war, quitting when I was down over $8,000. One more time that Antonio managed to beat me!

A few months later, I was deep into the World Poker Tour's Commerce championship when Antonio won it. To follow that up, he made it deep into the next day's WPT Invitational, which was—surprise!—won by one of his best friends, the aforementioned Phil Laak. I'm sure they had a great celebration! They certainly managed to impress me, and the next thing I knew Laak was going out with the famous actress (and accomplished poker player) Jennifer Tilly.

Later, I was at the final table when Antonio won his first WSOP (World Series of Poker) bracelet, in 2004. In fact, I finally landed my roundhouse on him that day when I moved him all-in with my K-K to his Q-Q. After a flop of Jc-9c-7c (I had the Kc), I was feeling really good. And even when the Qc came off—making him trips, but me a flush—I knew that I was a 3-to-1 favorite to win the pot! He needed one of three jacks, three nines, or three sevens or the one remaining queen on the last card to win the pot—10 wins to my 34 wins. But alas for me, the last card was a nine, and my roundhouse, although planted squarely, didn't knock Antonio out. I had him all-in again a few minutes later, this time with my Q-5 versus his A-J. This time I was a 2.5-to-1 underdog, and I lost again.

I finally exacted a measure of revenge in NBC's National Heads-Up Poker Championship in 2005, when I beat Antonio in the final four. But that battle, too, was fiercely fought to the bitter end. My roundhouse punch this time was my set of fours versus his top pair, with a board of K-4-3 (my 4-4 versus his K-J). This time he didn't wriggle out, and I went on to take that title. I look forward to many more of these confrontations with Antonio.

In 2004 and 2005, I have been out with Antonio for a few more Dom-fests, notably at the Top of the Mark, Light (the still red-hot Vegas bar in the Bellagio), and Pure (a new white-hot Vegas bar at Caesar's Palace). Our last few Vegas excursions usually involved Chris "Jesus" Ferguson, Annie Duke, Phil Gordon, Marcel Luske, and any other poker player ready for a night out. This magician knows how to have a good time. And with one WPT title and one WSOP title under his belt, this magician knows how to play poker!

Phil Hellmuth Jr. is a nine-time World Champion and author of Play Poker Like the Pros.

PHIL HELLMUTH, JR.

CHAPTER SIX

Preflop Strategy

JUMPING IN

I remember like it was yesterday the first time I sat down at a poker table in a casino. I was totally juiced to have those cards dealt to me across the green felt. The anticipation of peeking at my two little down cards not knowing what surprises they had in store for me was electric. My adrenaline was pumping, and I was, of course, more than a little nervous. It did not take long for me to settle down, though.

I long ago learned to take that adrenaline rush and channel it

Antonio's victory at Commerce Casino's 2004 L.A. Poker Classic.

into positive energy. I use it to stay alert and focused at the challenge at hand. Then I relax and play my game. If you are going to play poker, you should enjoy it. So take any of that nervous energy you may have and put it to work for you.

A WORD ABOUT BLINDS

In Hold 'Em, there are always two forced bets—which are called blinds—before the cards are dealt. The first player to the left of the button is the small blind and typically puts in a half bet. The second player to the left of the button is the big blind and always puts in a full bet. The button then rotates clockwise with every new deal so that everyone gets his fair turn in the blinds.

In the first round of betting of each hand, the player to the immediate left of the blinds is the first to act. He is referred to as being *under the gun*. The blinds will act last. If no one has raised, the small blind will often stay in since it will only cost him a half bet to see a flop. The big blind has the option of checking or raising because his full bet is already in the pot.

In each subsequent round of betting, the small blind will be the first to act if he is still in the pot. The player on the button (if he is still in the hand) will always be the last to act in the subsequent betting rounds. As I have mentioned before, Hold 'Em is a positional game. Thus, the button has the advantage of acting last and the benefit of seeing how everyone else acts before him on every single betting round.

If you are playing $10–$20 Limit Hold 'Em, $10 is the amount of a full bet for both the first betting round and the round of betting after the flop. Subsequent rounds (after the turn and the river) will have $20 bets. Typically, betting will be capped at three raises per round unless only two players are left, in which case the raises will be unlimited. In a $10–$20 game, the blinds would then be $5 and $10, representing a half bet and a full bet for the first round.

Now, let's saying you are playing $10–$20 No Limit Hold 'Em. The blinds would now be $10 and $20. Since the betting amounts are unlimited during any round, the name of the game represents the blind amounts. Minimum bets in this game for all rounds would be $20, and the minimum raises would be an amount equal to the last bet or raise. For example, suppose three players see a flop. The first player to act bets $25, which is $5 over the minimum bet allowed. If the next player wants to raise, he must raise at least $25. Suppose he raises $50 and makes it $75 to go. It will now cost the third player $75 to call; and if he wants to raise, he must raise at least $50.

While we will learn shortly about stealing blinds, the nature of the game in relation to the amount of the blinds will go a long way in determining whether the blinds are worth stealing. If you are playing a $1–$2 no-limit game with not much preflop action but a lot of postflop action, with average bets at least five times the big blind, then it does not make sense to steal blinds. Try to see some flops cheaply and give yourself the chance to win some big pots when you hit the flop. Conversely, if you are playing a game in which the blinds are more expensive and the players are conservative, then you may want to be more aggressive in stealing blinds.

Many players get caught up in the concept of defending their blinds. If you are playing Limit Hold 'Em, you certainly do not want a player in late position believing he can steal your blind any time he wants. However, I see many inexperienced players squander too many chips worrying about their blinds. When you are in the blinds, you have to remember that you are out of position. Even though you are acting last preflop, you are going to be acting first in each subsequent betting round. That is a very tough position to be in—especially in no-limit play. In no-limit play, it is essentially useless to try to defend your blinds. Not only are you going to be out of position, the amount of the blinds is typically a much smaller percentage of an average pot when compared to Limit Hold 'Em.

Unless I put the button on a total steal, I will even fold ace rag from the blinds. Do you really want to be playing ace rag from early position postflop in no-limit play? For the most part, you will be much better off in No Limit Hold 'Em if you just look at the blinds as the cost of doing business.

In fact, the blinds are your cost of entry to the game. When you first sit down to a table already in progress, you will have two choices. You can wait for your turn in the big blind to begin playing, or you can post a big blind out of position so you can start playing immediately. Unless you happen to sit down in late position, it usually makes sense to wait for the big blind to reach you. Regardless of what you do now, you are going to have to post the blinds when they reach you anyway, so why not wait? If you are in early position, it does not make sense to pay for the privilege of playing out of position—especially since you will have to post your turn in the blinds real soon. Posting a blind in early position sends a signal to the rest of the table that an inexperienced player just joined the game.

STARTING OUT

Whenever you sit down to a new table, I would suggest that you play fewer hands. Take the time to observe and see what type of game you are in and what kind of players you are up against so you can implement the optimal strategy for this game. For beginning or less-experienced players, I would suggest that you err on the side of being conservative with your starting-hand requirements. This will minimize your risk as you try to learn about your opponents and get accustomed to the table. Additionally, if you are new to No Limit Hold 'Em, I would suggest that you play with a short stack. This will help minimize your losses and make your decision-making process easier. With a short stack in a no-limit game, there will be more of an emphasis on preflop play, which is generally easier for beginning players to play than postflop.

As you gain more experience, you should expand your starting requirements. As you get better, you will learn to play more hands profitably. As you continue to improve, you will want to mix up your play to make it unpredictable and to keep your opponents from getting a read on you. In other words, beginning players should play more by the book. As with most pursuits in life, you have to learn the basic guidelines before you start to bend them. As you get more experienced in Hold 'Em, you will soon find that there is a lot to gain by mixing up your play and not playing by the book. Poker is a game of imperfect information. You want to spread as much misinformation as you can about your play.

The most important factor in deciding what hands to play is position. The later you act, the more hands you can play. Conversely, when you are in early position, you will need a strong hand to enter the action. In a typical full-table game, there are three general starting positions after the blinds: early, middle, and late. As a general rule, positions one and two to the left of the button are the blinds, positions three through five are the early positions, positions six through eight the middle positions, and positions nine and ten (ten being the button) the late positions.

EARLY POSITION IN NO-LIMIT PLAY

From early position, I am only going to enter the pot with a strong hand and will typically only raise with very strong hands. The hands I will raise with are A-A, A-K, and K-K. Depending on how tight the table is, I may also raise with Q-Q, A-Q suited, and A-J suited. If I am going to raise from early position, I will generally raise three times the amount of the big blind. If you consistently raise the same amount, you end up giving away less information about your hand than if you always raise more with A-A. I will limp in with any medium or low pair. While I will never raise from early position with small pocket pairs, I will call a moderate raise because I can win a big pot if I hit my set on the flop.

Hands to be careful with in early position include A-Q off-suit, A-J offsuit, K-Q, J-10 suited, and any other suited connectors. I will generally throw these hands away unless I am playing with some very weak players. The reason is that these hands are very difficult to play out of position. Of all of these borderline hands, the ones I like the best in no-limit play are the bigger suited connectors. If I think I can get in cheap with these hands, I will because I can win big pots with them. Otherwise, I will toss them in the muck with the rest of these borderline hands.

EARLY POSITION IN LIMIT PLAY

There are two big differences between no-limit play and limit play when making early position decisions. First, there is no decision to be made as to how much you want to raise. The only decision to make is if you want to raise, because the amount you can raise is limited by the game to one times the amount of the big blind. Next, you can generally play more of the borderline hands, because you do not have to worry about significant raises behind you. In limit play, you can play hands like A-Q offsuit, A-J offsuit, or K-Q. In fact, you may even want to raise with these hands. The reason these hands have more value in limit play is that they will not get you in as much trouble. For example, say you play A-Q and get one raiser behind you. You know this player can be fairly aggressive and does not need a premium hand to raise. You call, and the flop brings an ace. If you want to check and call all the way to a showdown, you know the maximum amount this hand could cost you. If, on the other hand, you were playing No Limit Hold 'Em, you could lose a lot of money if you are up against A-K or two pair.

By the same logic, suited connectors do not have the same upside in limit play as they do in no-limit play, because you cannot trap your opponents for a huge pot if you flop a monster hand.

MIDDLE POSITION

In middle position, a lot will depend on the action in front of you. If no one has raised, you can play all of the hands that you would have played from early position. In addition, you can open up your starting requirements. I would limp in now with hands like A-10, K-J, Q-10, or J-10 suited. If there has been a limper or two, I would call with hands like A-x suited (x being any card nine or lower) or suited connectors below J-10. I may even play J-9 suited. If there have not been any limpers, I'd probably fold these hands as they play better multihanded. If a couple of players have limped in front of me, I'm going to play two gap-suited cards. Those are hands like 7-10 suited or 6-9 suited. I like to play a lot of hands if I can see the flop cheaply. I personally like to dance and maneuver as much as I can, but there is certainly nothing wrong with folding two gap-suited cards here—especially if you are inexperienced. There are still too many people to act behind you, and you do not have that good a position yet.

With middle position, you must also know the nature of your opponents behind you. If I have very aggressive players acting behind me, I will be more cautious from middle position and may even play it just like early position. With tight players behind me who do not know how to use their late-position advantage, I will play middle position more aggressively. Say, for example, you have J-10 suited in middle position and one player has limped in front of you. If there is a very aggressive player behind you, one who likes to raise with marginal hands once a pot develops, then just limp in. If, on the other hand, there are only very tight players behind you, you may want to raise. By doing this, you will force out some otherwise playable hands, giving you position after the flop. If you do get called or raised by one of these tight players, then you know you are in trouble to a player who has position on you.

LATE POSITION

Here is where the action is. Hold 'Em is a positional game, and late position is primo real estate. If location is everything in real estate, position is everything in Hold 'Em. You always want to try and play within position. From late position, the game completely opens up. Of course, from here you can play every hand that is playable from early and middle position. You can even raise with some of the more marginal hands. Hands like K-J, Q-10, and K-10 are very playable. If no one has yet raised, I may even bump it up with those hands. There are two critical points to playing hands like these. First, you will have position postflop, and you are in excellent shape to take down pots if you get any piece of it and your opponents miss. The next and more critical point is that you have to have the discipline to get away from these hands if you are beat—even if you have top pair. For example, say you call a raise from late position with K-10 suited. The flop comes K-9-4 rainbow. The initial raiser bets, you raise, and he reraises. It's time to get rid of your hand. Your opponent may have A-K, K-Q, K-J, or even a set of kings or nines. Unless you know this opponent to be ultraaggressive, anyone playing his hand that strongly from early position has you beat. In a no-limit game, you do not want to lose big pots with nothing but top pair. In limit play, it is a little easier just to call down to the river, knowing that the most you can lose is three bets.

You want to be in control from late position. At this point, you are playing your opponents more than you are playing your cards. This is especially true in no-limit play, where it is much easier to chase out weak or even marginal hands. That's why your starting requirements can be loosened quite a bit. I will play A-x suited and two gap-suited cards, such as 5-8 and 4-7. From late position, I can win a lot of pots with these hands. For instance, say there are a couple of limpers in early position and I call from the button with 4-7 of spades. The flop comes 9-5-4 with one spade. One of the early position players bet, and the action is on me. I know this flop did not help him, but I just call here. Why? Because I know I still have position on him for the next two rounds of betting. Also, by calling, I will make him think I have something. Now, say the turn brings the three of spades. I now have a flush draw, a gut-shot straight draw, and my one pair may even be good. I am in excellent position to make a play at my opponent no matter what he does. Even if that turn card did not help me, I can make a play as long as it did not help my opponent. In fact, the more aggressive I am in late position, the easier it is to take these pots. If my opponents know that I will play a lot of hands from late position, then it is hard for them to put me on a hand, and there is no way they will know if those marginal flops help me.

To reiterate, Hold 'Em is a positional game. Never forget that when you are making your preflop decisions. It is very tempting for beginning players to bet marginal hands out of position because they are anxious to get into the action. This is especially true if you have not seen anything worth playing in quite a while. If you go a couple of rounds looking at cards like 4-9 offsuit, all of a sudden Q-10 looks good. Well, if you are in early position in an aggressive game, Q-10 is not any good. Whenever you feel the temptation to play one of these hands out of position, keep in mind that there are still a number of players to act behind you. And if you manage to see a flop, you still have three more betting rounds to navigate, and you will be out of position for each of them. Be patient and wait for favorable position before making your moves.

ISOLATING FROM LATE POSITION

When you have a hand that plays better heads-up than in a multi-way pot, you ideally want to isolate one opponent. What do I mean by isolation? You isolate an opponent by chasing everyone else out of the pot so that you can play a pot heads-up with one opponent. This increases your chances of winning when you have a made hand as opposed to a drawing hand.

For example, say you are on the button and everyone folds to the player in front of you. You know him to be an aggressive player, and sure enough he raises. You know that there is a wide range of hands that he would raise with here. You look down and see a pair of nines. Reraise here. By doing so, you can get the blinds to fold everything but a premium hand, since they would have to call a raise and a reraise. You now are now one on one with an opponent you have position on. There is a good chance that you are ahead right now because he could be playing any suited connector, an ace, two paint cards, or a smaller pair. Plus, you have position. That is a tremendous advantage, especially since by reraising you have represented a strong hand. For example, say the flop comes down A-K-4, which at first glance looks bad for you. If your opponent checks, go ahead and bet. Unless he has K-K, 4-4, or an ace, he is going to have to fold. By being aggressive preflop, you have set up a position bet postflop. It is critical to your success to be aggressive when you have position and opportunity.

When you have the opportunity to isolate an opponent pre-flop with a decent, but not great, heads-up hand, do so. You eliminate opponents from even seeing a flop, and you have position on your one opponent. You have now given yourself two chances to win: either you hit the flop, or a scary flop comes that your opponent has to check. If you had just called preflop, your opponent may sense your vulnerability and bet the scary flop himself even though it did not help him. Then you would have been the one forced to fold. By being aggressive preflop, you have taken the lead in this hand. One caveat here: In no-limit play, you have to proceed a bit more cautiously. Whenever you reraise, there is the chance that an opponent will reraise you. In limit play, you know how much that will be. In no-limit play, you do not. So let's take another look at this preflop play. If you reraise with your pocket nines and your opponent raises again, there is an excellent chance that your opponent has you dominated with a bigger pair. In limit play, it still is worthwhile to call one bet and see a flop. However, if your opponent reraised, say, two or three times your raise in this situation, you should fold. Now, if you had just called you would have been able to see a flop—however, you would have failed to taken the lead in the betting, and your opponent is likely to bet a scary flop. Thus, what you do in this situation in no-limit play really comes down to experience and your feel for the game and your opponent. This is a perfect example of some of the subtle differences in limit and no-limit play. While there are no absolutes in poker, you are almost always correct in raising in this situation in limit play. However, in no-limit play, the situation calls for more analysis of the entire situation, and how you proceed is really going to come down to your gut feeling based on everything you have observed so far at the table. Be careful who and when you try to isolate. As powerful of a tool as it is, you have to make sure you are not isolating a hand that dominates you. If a tight player raises from early position, you do not want to isolate him with those pair of nines. Your opponent either has you dominated with a bigger pair or has something like A-K that will sabotage any chance you have of playing the scary flop.

STEALING THE BLINDS FROM LATE POSITION

Stealing the blinds from late position comes up when everyone folds to a player in late position, who then has the opportunity to make a bet to force the blinds to fold and thus scoop the pot. For example, say you are on the button and everyone folds to you. You look down and see 7-2 offsuit. At this point, it really does not matter what cards you are holding. If you make a big bet here, the blinds will be forced to call out of position. That's a tough call for them to make without decent starting hands. That is why stealing the blinds is a popular move. I would offer a couple of words of caution about this move.

First, because it is such a popular move, most everyone will be on to it. You have to know your opponents in the blinds. Are they likely to defend their blinds or not? Even a weak opponent may get tired of you stealing his blind at every opportunity. More important, however, is to consider how big the blinds are in relation to the game. If you are playing $1–$2 No Limit Hold 'Em where the average pot is over $30, then there is not much incentive to steal the blinds. You never want to risk a lot to win a little. If the average preflop raise is $10 in that $1–$2 game, is it really worth betting $10 to try to steal $3 with 7-2 offsuit? Save that $10 to put to use in a better situation.

SLOW-PLAYING PREFLOP

From early or middle position, I will rarely slow-play a strong hand such as A-A or K-K. These hands play best heads-up, and I do not want too many limpers coming in. Besides, if I consistently raise from this position with all of my strong hands, opponents will have a hard time putting me on aces or kings. The only time I may slow-play big pairs in early position is if I know I have an aggressive player behind me who likes to raise. If he raises, then I can come over the top with a big reraise.

In late position, what you do is really going to depend on your reputation. I will raise with aces or kings in late position 99 percent of the time because it will look suspicious if I just limped. My opponents are used to me raising from late position. If you limp a lot in late position, then you can occasionally limp in with pocket aces or kings if no one has entered the pot before you. If everyone folds to you on the button, go ahead and limp in, since you may get to see the flop heads-up anyway (or three-handed, at the most). You may even get one of the blinds to raise. Do not always make this move, though. When everyone folds to you on the button and you raise, your hand is already well hidden. The blinds can easily put you on a positional raise. If that is the case, there are a lot of hands that you can raise with from that position.

ADDITIONAL CONSIDERATIONS

If you are playing no limit, it is extremely important to know your opponents and their tendencies. When you enter a pot preflop, you want to either win the pot or at least see a flop. The last thing you want to do is contribute to a hand, only to fold before you even get to see a flop. In limit play, you know the maximum you can be raised, and your chances of at least seeing a flop are much greater.

In no-limit play, however, you can be pushed off a hand (or you can push an opponent off a hand) with one big bet. That's why you need to know which players will make those big bets preflop and with which hands. I am not going to raise with A-Q suited from early position if I know I am sure to get reraised from a player behind me. This can get very expensive. If I raise from early position, I am typically going to bring it in for three times the amount of the big blind. Now, if I get reraised, that amount is going to be at least six times the big blind. I am much better off limping in and calling a raise that's three times the big blind. Every time you make a bet or raise, think about what you are trying to accomplish. All of your moves should be purposeful based on the entire situation. You do not want to be betting your cards blindly.

You must also consider the relative stack sizes of your opponents. Against a very aggressive player with a large stack, you are not going to want to raise him unless you have a very strong hand. Every time you raise, you sweeten the pot and open the door for him to reraise you in a big way. Weaker players with short stacks are a different matter: you can push them around more often.

CHAPTER SEVEN

Postflop Play

If you have followed the advice in the previous chapter, then you are going to avoid a lot of problems that can arise after the flop. That is, you will not find yourself out of position with a marginal hand. If you are in early position, you should have started with a strong hand, and the nature of the flop will largely determine how you play. If you are in late position, then the hands you could be holding are varied. Now, both the nature of the flop and what your opponent(s) do will each play a significant role in your actions. Let's look first at some general postflop considerations before getting into some specific situations.

Antonio with three close friends on an average Friday night.

After the flop is not the time to be tentative. Be smart, but be aggressive. If I led the betting before the flop, I will try to lead after the flop. For example, say I raised in early position preflop with Ad-Kd, and I got one caller. The flop comes 10c-6h-4h. While this does not help me, there is a good chance it will not help my opponent, either. How do I know whether it helped my opponent? Well, I don't. At least not right away. However, let's look at my options here and see which one is more likely to help me gain information and maximize my winnings.

I have two choices here. I can bet or check. Let's look at betting first. If I bet out, my opponent has three choices. He can fold, call, or raise. Since I raised preflop from early position, my opponent has to give me credit for a premium hand. As we learned in the previous chapter, I consistently raise with any premium hand in early position. Therefore, my opponent will not know which premium hand I hold. If he does not have a pocket pair and missed the flop, he knows he has to be behind here, and there is a good chance he will fold to my bet. That's fine with me. I will gladly take the pot with ace high rather than give my opponent a chance to draw out. Plus, I have now gained some information on my opponent. He gave up on this hand when he missed the flop.

Now, let's suppose my opponent called preflop with pocket nines. If I bet the flop, he still does not know what premium hand I have. I could still have him dominated with any higher pair. But he also knows that I may have a hand like A-K, A-Q, or A-J, which would put him ahead of me. So, with 9-9, he will most likely either call or raise. By raising, he hopes to find out whether I have a hand or was being aggressive. (If I was him, I would consider raising. If I am ahead, I want to protect my hand. If I am behind, I want to find out as soon as possible.)

Now let's look at what he would do with a hand like A-10 or Ah-Jh. With the first hand, he has top pair with top kicker. With the second hand, he has the nut flush draw. With both of these hands, he should consider raising. By raising, he puts me on the defensive and finds out some information. With the flush draw on board, a good player knows that I will reraise with an overpair in order to protect my hand. If I do not have an overpair, there is a good chance I will fold. Now, with the flush draw, he may want to just call and take another card, especially in no limit. With the nut-flush draw, give yourself a chance to see another card rather than risk a big reraise that forces you out of the hand.

So let's see what I have found out by betting. First, if my opponent folds, he is willing to throw away his hand to a bet on a nonscary board. If he calls, I am most likely behind or my opponent has a flush draw. However, I still have a chance to outdraw him. But I have gained valuable information. If I get an overcard on the turn that does not fill the flush, I can bet again, and he may be forced to fold even with a better hand, such as nines. Finally, if my opponent raises, I have to throw my hand away in no-limit play. The risk-reward ratio is just not worth it. If he has a set or a hand such as A-10, I am in a lot of trouble. I could get in a lot of trouble if I was drawing dead and hit top pair on the river. In limit play, the analysis is different. If he has a pocket pair, I am getting correct pot odds to call one more bet here. I now have a good idea of what I am up against, however, and can act accordingly on the turn.

Now let's look at one other scenario that shows why it's important to lead out betting after this flop. If my opponent has a hand like Qs-Js, I have the best hand right now. Yet if I check, I open the door for him to take a stab at the pot. It is very difficult to play out of position, so instead of giving him an opportunity to steal from me, I am going to bet out. If I check and he bets, then my only options are folding (which means I lose the pot) or raising (which means I am now forced to commit more chips than I would have if I had bet out in the first place). Calling is not really an option here because I would be committing chips without finding out any information. The bottom line is that if I raised preflop and am in a heads-up pot, I am going to bet out postflop almost every single time.

Now let's look at what can happen if I check the flop. If I check this flop, I show weakness. Why is that? Well, if he has been paying attention, he knows that I am an aggressive bettor and would not slow-play a top pair with a flush draw on board. The only hand he might be worried about is top set, but I would not even slow-play that. I almost always bet out my big hands. So, by checking, I signal that I missed the flop, and I now give him the opportunity to lead the betting. If he takes that lead—which he should—I am now on the defensive. Yeah, I have overcards and may be getting correct pot odds to call, but now I have no idea what he has. Furthermore, if he is on a flush draw with that Ah-Jh hand, I have just given him a free card. Now, what happens if the Kh comes on the turn? I am likely to bet into the nut flush with my top pair because I have no idea what he has.

So, by betting out this flop, I accomplish two things. First, I have given myself a chance to win the pot right there. Next, even if I get called or raised, I gain information that can help me win the pot on a later street or save me money. If I had checked, I give my opponent the chance to take the lead in betting. Whether he does or doesn't, it will be hard for me to ascertain any information. Poker is a game of imperfect information. You can always gain more information from an opponent by betting into him than you can by checking into him. This does not mean that you should always bet into an opponent. Be aggressive, but be smart.

For example, say I raised preflop from early position with

that same Ad-Kd, but this time I get three callers. The flop comes 7c-8c-9h. This is a horrible flop for me. I have nothing but two overcards, and there is a good chance one of my opponents has a made hand or at least a very good draw. There is nothing to be gained by me betting out here. I will check and fold to any bet. Everything in poker is situational. Stay focused, and stay on top of the unique nature of each hand. Remember, each hand unfolds like its very own movie script. How I play A-K after the flop in early position will depend not only on what the flop is, but will also depend on how many opponents I face, what they are likely to have, my read of my opponents, and my own table image.

SIZE OF CHIP STACK

The size of your chip stack compared to your opponents is a huge consideration in no-limit play. You do not want to get too aggressive and jeopardize your stack. For example, say you start with A-K in late position preflop. A tight middle-position player with a huge stack open raised. You should just call in that situation. By calling, you get to see a flop, and then you can reevaluate. Also, by calling, you hide the value of your hand. So let's say you called an $80 preflop bet, and now you see a flop heads-up. Each of you is sitting on a $4,000 stack in a $10–$20 no-limit game. The flop comes A-7-2. This appears to be a good flop for you. Your opponent bets out $200. This is a very tempting hand to reraise, yet I would just smooth-call here.

If you raise here, there are not many hands he can have that he can call you with. Most likely, you are only going to get called by a better hand. Your best hope is that he has A-Q or A-J. If you do in fact have the best hand, you have much better equity in letting your opponent continue to do your betting for you. Even if he has nothing, he may try to bluff you on the turn. When you are heads-up, there is not as big a premium on raising. In a multi-way pot, you need to chase out drawing hands or even smaller pairs. With too many people in the pot, there is greater uncertainty.

You also want to avoid getting overly aggressive with top pair. You never want to go broke with top pair after the flop. The only time you would get very aggressive with top pair postflop is if a lot of money went in preflop and it is worth your while to take it down. Even then, you have to be careful going up against a large stack.

At a recent game I was playing, I witnessed the following hand. The blinds were $10–$20, there was a three-times-the-big-blind raise from early position, and two players called. The flop came Q-9-6 rainbow. The early position raiser moved all-in. The next player to act immediately called. Now, my friend Noah Boeken was sitting on the button with pocket sixes. He had flopped a set, yet he was now debating whether to call. I think he was more worried about the player who called than the initial raiser. I should point out that neither of the other players were very good. After a few seconds, Noah decided to call and the cards were turned over. The initial raiser had A-Q for top pair, and the second player had J-10 for an open-end straight draw. Noah had made an excellent call, because he was an overwhelming favorite to win the hand. Noah's hand held up, and he scooped a big pot.

The initial raiser made a big mistake by committing all of his chips when he was out of position and all he had was top pair. He committed all of his chips when there were two other players in the pot with larger stacks. If he wanted to chase out drawing hands, I would normally say that he could have accomplished the same thing without risking so much. Yet Player 2 clearly would have called with his straight draw, since he called the all-in bet without any hesitation. That, however, was a terrible call. At the time he called, Player 2 was a 3-to-1 underdog and was only getting slightly better than 2-to-1 odds to play. That is not smart poker.

When making a bet or raise, always think of what you are trying to accomplish. If you want to chase people out, then come up with the right amount to bet that will get the job done without going overboard. If a $400 bet will have the same effect as a $1,000 bet, why risk that extra $600. Never risk more than you need to. If you want callers, then bet the amount that an opponent is likely to call.

POSITION

The reason you use position preflop is that you will now have position postflop (as well as on the turn and the river). By the same token, the reason you only play strong hands out of position preflop is because you will be out of position postflop. There will be a lot of what I call *orphan flops.* These are flops that do not help anyone. When you have position, you will have the benefit of having watched what everyone else did. If no one makes a play for the pot, you can. Even if someone does make a play, you can still trump them. What do I mean by that? Say a player raises from early position and you call from the button with J-10 suited. You see a flop heads-up and it comes 8-7-2 rainbow. You have a gutshot straight draw, a back-door flush draw, and two overcards. At the moment, though, all you have is jack high. You know you most likely do not have the best hand right now, but you also do not think that this flop helped your opponent.

Your opponent bets out after the flop as most players will do when they raise preflop. You now have three choices. You can fold, call, or raise. I would not fold here, as your position is a powerful weapon. I may implement a semi-bluff raise or just smooth-call here, depending on my opponent. With a number of outs here, a semi-bluff is a good move. It could win you the pot right away. If your opponent calls or raises, he may have an overpair, and you know you need to slow down. You could also just call here. This buys you another card and also sends a message. Even if the turn does not help you, you can take the hand down with an aggressive move on the turn, as long as the turn does not help your opponent.

With J-10, there are so many cards that can peel off the turn that are good for you. Not only are there the cards that hit your hand, but there are also many others that will scare your opponent. Let's say your opponent has A-8, which is a great hand for that flop. He bets the flop and you call. Now, a 7, a 9, a 10, a jack, a queen, and a king are all good cards for you. He will most likely check the turn with one of those cards, and you can bet out (even with a card like the king that did not help you). Your opponent should then fold here. Even if he is stubborn and calls, you always have the river to go for it again. This situation is great for you even when your opponent hits a great flop with his A-8. Now imagine if you call the flop and your opponent has nothing. (Say he started with A-Q). He will almost never take another stab at it if he misses the turn. Stu Ungar once said in a very famous quote, "Most people will fire one bullet, but not many will fire two or three."

That is the value of having position. You can call bets on the flop with every intention of taking it on the turn if your opponent does not have anything.

CHECK-RAISE BLUFFS

There are ways you can use early position to your advantage. A check-raise bluff is a powerful weapon that is available to players in early position. It is a great way to counteract an aggressive opponent who uses position effectively. If you know you are up against an opponent who will use his position to make a move, let him. Once he does, then you can spring a check-raise bluff on him. In order to maximize the chances of your check-raise bluff working, it has to be believable to your opponent. Let me offer a couple of ideal situations to try this.

First, say you are able to see a flop cheaply from the big blind while holding 8-10. The flop is one of those orphan flops that comes 9-4-2. This is a flop that may not have helped anybody. In fact, from the other players' perspective, it is most likely to help you, since the range of hands you could be playing in the big blind is wide. If you bet out, though, your opponents may think you are trying to steal the orphan flop. If you check-raise, however, your opponents are much more likely to give you credit for a hand. Even if they do think you are bluffing, it will be hard for them to call unless they have a hand.

Another ideal situation occurs when you open-raise from early position with a hand such as K-Q suited. You only get one caller, and the flop comes A-8-3. Even though this did not help you, you are in ideal position to represent a big ace. If you have an opponent who loves to bet position, then check-raise him here. Most people check-raise when they have monsters. Use that to your advantage and check-raise with nothing. Go ahead and give it a whirl, and see how well it works.

Now let's look at some specific situations.

PLAYING OVERPAIRS

Again, be aggressive, but be smart. If I have an overpair after the flop, I am most likely going to bet or raise after the flop. If I am in early position with 10-10, J-J, Q-Q, K-K, or A-A, remember that I would have raised preflop to narrow the field. If I get a caller or two and the flop comes 9-7-2 rainbow, I am going to bet out. There is not much to be gained by slow-playing here. Say I have Q-Q and two opponents. I am vulnerable to any ace or king or a hand like J-10 that has an inside straight draw. Why give my opponents a chance to draw out on me? If they want to try to draw out, let them pay for it. Now, if I have A-A here, I may slow-play. The potential hands that could beat me are much narrower, so I will try to trap an opponent. If I am playing No Limit Hold 'Em, I may be able to take an opponent for a good amount of money if he is holding a hand such as A-K and a king hits on the turn.

Now, let's look at a different situation. A tight opponent raises from early position preflop. I call in late position with my J-J. The flop comes 10-8-3 rainbow. My opponent bets out. What do I do? I know my opponent has a premium hand, but I do not know which one. He could have a bigger pair than me, in which case I am way behind and should give up on the hand. He could, however, be playing aggressive with A-K or A-Q. Remember, it pays to be aggressive. A good opponent knows this as well as I do. He also could have a hand like A-10, which would be great for me. So what is my move? I am not going to fold this hand with an overpair, so I can either call or raise. Remember when I said before that you learn more from betting into an opponent than checking. Well, the same is true here. If I call, I will still be in the dark about my opponent. But if I raise, I take control of the betting and put my opponent on the defensive. If my opponent was playing A-Q, he will probably fold, which keeps him from drawing out on me. If he has A-10, he will probably call, which gives me more money in the pot; I also have a pretty good idea that I have him beat. If he has A-A or K-K, he my call or reraise. If he does reraise, I know I am in trouble. However, by raising in this position instead of just calling, I take control of the betting and give myself a chance to win the pot or gain more information.

PLAYING TOP PAIR

I am always aggressive when I flop top pair. I play aggressively here for a number of reasons. First, I do not want anyone outdrawing me. If someone wants to play to draw, it will cost them. I want to narrow the field so that my hand holds up. Next, I want to increase the pot. Since there is a good chance I have the best hand here, I want to get some money in the pot. I tend not to get too tricky here. If I am consistently aggressive, I am not giving away my hand since it will be hard for my opponent to read me. Finally, I want information. If my hand is in trouble, I want to find out about it. Remember, you can find out more information by betting than checking.

MIDDLE PAIR

When you are playing No Limit Hold 'Em, middle pairs require more finesse. A lot will depend on your feel for the game and your opponents. If you are confident that you have the best hand, go ahead and make a decent-sized bet in order to win the pot and keep opponents from drawing out on you. If someone bets into you or raises you, you are going to have to make a determination about what your opponent has and what he is likely to be holding. In limit play, you can always call an opponent down to the river when you are unsure of his hand and you know exactly how many bets it will cost you. In no-limit play, you do not want to get sucked into a pot when you are behind. You have no idea how much this hand will cost you on the turn or the river if you want to see it to the end. However, you also do not want other players feeling they can push you around. What you do will depend on your table image, who your opponent is, and what he is likely to have. With experience, you should get more comfortable knowing what to do in these situations and to trust your judgments. Always maintain your focus at the table and these decisions will get easier. When I say to maintain your focus, I am not just talking about your observations of other players. Stay attuned to your own table image and what everyone's likely perception of you is. Remember that your opponent will have tough decisions to make also. By keeping your play unpredictable and being aggressive, you put your opponent on the defensive and make it tough for him to make correct decisions.

FLOPPING A SET

Flopping a set is very sexy. Holding a pocket pair with anticipation and then to see the flop bring another card of your rank is a very empowering feeling. It's intoxicating. In fact, it is so intoxicating that players tend to get too infatuated with this hand. They want to savior the feeling, so they slow-play. This is the wrong move. I always bet out sets. If you have been consistently aggressive about playing your flops the correct way, you will actually be giving away less information by betting out or raising. If you slow-play or check-raise, you will be giving your hand away, and you will not get any more action. In addition, depending on the nature of the flop, you do not want to give anybody free cards to out draw you. If there is a flush or a straight draw on board, make your opponents pay to chase you.

FLOPPING A MONSTER

It does not happen often, but occasionally you will flop a full house, the nut flush, or the nut straight. The natural inclination when you flop these monster hands is to check. You want to slow-play in order to hide the value of your hand and to give your opponents time to catch something. If you are up against a loose aggressive opponent, this is not a bad strategy. Let them do your betting for you. However, more experienced players will suspect your hand if you slow-play. Again, if you have been playing aggressive poker, you will not be giving anything away by betting out with a monster.

Personally, I don't like to slow-play flops even if I hit a monster. I am not a big fan of slow-playing anything. Of course, because I am consistently aggressive, my opponents are less likely to put me on a monster. There is also another reason not to slow-play the flop. You run the risk of cutting off all the action and costing yourself money. Let me offer you an example of what I am talking about. Say you have 9-10 of clubs and your opponent has 6-6 and the board comes 6-7-8 with two hearts. You try to slow-play your nut straight and check. Your opponent checks as well, hoping to trap you with his set. Now a very bad thing can happen. The turn can bring a scare card. A 4, a 5, a 9, a 10, or any heart will stop the action on the turn. You don't want to take that chance. You want to bet when you flop the nuts, and you have to hope your opponents have something, too.

Knowing your opponents is key to maximizing your profit here. If you are up against a loose, passive player who will call you down with anything, then bet the maximum amount that he will call. This is another example of why it is so critical in no-limit play to understand your opponent's game. Monster hands only come around so often. The ability to take full advantage of them will prove instrumental to building your bankroll. In limit play, the amount you can bet is, of course, capped by the appropriate limits. In no-limit play, there is a no such barrier. The question then becomes one of how much you should bet in order to maximize profits. If you have been paying attention, you should know what to do. That is, you will know whether to slow-play or play aggressive, and how much your opponent(s) are likely to call.

PLAYING DRAWING HANDS

There are two times to play drawing hands: first, when you can draw for free or are at least getting correct pot odds to do so; and second, when you can semi-bluff with them. Let's look at drawing for free or when you are getting correct pot odds.

To determine if you are getting correct pot odds, you must know the amount of the pot, how much it will cost you, and the odds of making your hand. There are a couple of additional considerations as well. If you are going to pay to draw, you have to be sure that if you hit your hand, you are going to win. For instance, if you are holding 7s-8s and the board is 2c-9d-10d, you have an open-end straight draw. The problem is that you could hit your straight and easily end up with a losing hand. There are two diamonds on the board, so if the 6d shows up on the turn, filling your straight, it may make your opponent a flush. In addition, suppose the Js shows up on the turn. Again, you have hit your straight, but an opponent could easily have K-Q and trump you with a bigger straight. The bottom line is that this is not a good drawing hand for you even if you are getting correct pot odds. You should only play this hand if you can continue for free or very cheaply.

When you can draw for free, the question then becomes whether you should semi-bluff or not. Let's look at another example. A tight passive player open-raises in early position and you call on the button, holding Qd-Jd. The flop comes 2d-5c-8d. Your opponent checks. You are fairly confident he's holding A-K. At this point, he is ahead, but you have a flush draw. You can take a free card here and see if you hit your flush on the turn. The problem with doing that against a tight opponent is that unless the Ad or the Kd shows up on the turn, you are not going to get any more money out of this tight passive opponent. So, in this example, you are probably better off betting the flop and taking the pot down. If you do get called, you have two overcards and a flush draw, so you are still in very good shape. In addition, you can still take the pot on a later street if your opponent is playing A-K and never improves.

Again, knowing your opponent is so important. You would not want to semi-bluff against an opponent who loves to check-raise. The last thing you want to do with a drawing hand is pass on an opportunity for a free card by betting out, only to find yourself facing a big raise. If the raise is big enough, you may not even get to see another card after you have committed more money to the pot.

A Well-Grounded Antonio

by Annie Duke

I met Antonio for the first time on the set of the very first World Poker Tour commercial. Phil Hellmuth, Paul Darden, Chris Ferguson, and I were slated to be in the commercial, and Antonio was picked to be the dealer. I had no idea who this young, good-looking kid was, but right away I got such a good vibe from him. Antonio seemed like such a personable, funny, stand-up guy that I immediately started chatting with him. We became fast friends on that shoot and have been part of each other's lives ever since.

After that shoot, we kept in touch and started hanging out when we saw each other at tournaments. We would go out, and I was brought into his night-clubbing ways. There is no one on this planet who knows how to have a good time better than Antonio. But more than the good time, I saw how generous of spirit, time, and heart he was with all his friends. It just made me like him more.

In a world where young people can often lose their grounding, especially when success of the magnitude Antonio has achieved comes at such a young age, Antonio has never let his feet leave the ground. He is always grateful for what he has, always eager to help everyone around him. He treats everyone with respect and good humor. And, perhaps most important to me, he treats his family better than anyone I have ever seen.

So when UltimateBet.com came to me asking to add a member to Team UB, I pushed hard for Antonio. I knew he would represent the company well and work hard for its success. Team UB listened to me, and Antonio and I became more than just friends—we became business partners as well.

I have watched Antonio grow into an amazing poker player over the last few years and expect his success at the game and in life will only go up from here. I hope that the readers of this book will learn to respect and like him as much as I do through their reading of it. I know they will learn a hell of a lot.

Often called the top female player in the world, most players will agree that Annie Duke is one of the best players period.

CHAPTER EIGHT

Playing the Turn

The turn is where we separate the men from the boys, the women from the girls, and the players from the pretenders. As I alluded to earlier, an inexperienced player may fire one bullet, but a real player will fire at least two. What do I mean by that? Say, for example, you raise in early position with A-Q suited preflop. You get two callers and the flop comes 10-7-2 rainbow. This looks like a flop that may not have helped anyone, so you lead out betting after the flop. You get one player to fold, but the other player calls. The turn brings a king. What do you do? It is usually correct to fire another bullet at the pot here. Make another bet, and don't make it a wimpy one if you're playing No Limit

Hold 'Em. The turn is no place to show weakness. There will be times when you get burned by your aggression, but overall you will make money. That king can be a real scare card for someone playing a hand such as 9-10. Now, if in the example above a 4 came off the turn, it would probably be best to stop firing. If your opponent has a 10 in his hand, he is unlikely to fold to the non-scary 4.

The turn is where players' hands really shape up. If you have been paying attention, you should have a fairly good idea as to the strength of their hands by now. If the board has not helped you by this point, you have to know if it has helped your opponent. If you think he has a hand, then it is time to put on the brakes and not commit any more chips to this pot. If you believe the board has not helped your opponent, then you should maneuver for the pot. If your opponent is a tight player, then you should bet out in order to induce him to fold. If he is an aggressive player that will use position to his advantage and knows the board did not help you, either, then now may be the perfect time to try a check-raise bluff. A check-raise bluff projects a stronger hand than just betting into the pot.

For example, say you open-raise in middle position with Ks-Qs. You get one caller in late position. The flop comes 10-9-3 rainbow. You bet and your opponent calls. The turn brings an off suit 4. At this point, the board does not look dangerous at all. You still have a gut-shot straight draw and two overcards. Your opponent's call on the flop worries you, though. He may have a 10, a straight draw, or two overcards, or he may be setting you up to take the hand on the turn. Furthermore, your opponent is likely to know that this is not a good board for you as well. If you bet out, he may put you on a steal and raise. If you check, he may bet out to try to take the pot. If he does, then you can check-raise bluff, which will really put him on the defensive. At that point, he has to give you credit for a hand. If he calls, you know he has something. You still have outs, though, so the move is not a complete loss for you. Your hand could improve to a winner on the river.

The turn is where the price of poker gets more expensive. In limit play, the bets double. In no-limit play, the pot is usually larger, and this is when players want to put the squeeze on their opponents. Drawing hands have to be carefully evaluated. On the flop with two cards to come, your chances of hitting are greater. If you do not hit that card on the turn, however, your odds of making your hand decrease dramatically. Reevaluate your pot odds. Just because you chased the turn does not mean that you have to chase the river. Conversely, make your opponents pay if they want to continue drawing. Put pressure on them. Knowing your opponents, being aggressive, and using position are all still important on the turn. Let me describe a real-life example of a hand I recently played that illustrates how all of these elements come together on the turn.

I was playing $10–$20 No Limit Hold 'Em. A player in early position open-raised for three times the amount of the big blind. I called from late position with 7s-8s. My opponent was not very experienced, and I wanted to take advantage of my position. Suited connectors are a good hand to play in No Limit Hold 'Em from late position. We took the flop heads-up, and it came down 9d-8c-4c. My opponent checked and I made a pot-sized bet with middle pair. He called. Now, at this point I believed I had the best hand. I thought he most likely had a flush draw with two clubs. There was a chance, though, that he had a 9. The turn brings the 10s. Again my opponent checks. At this point, the pot is now big enough to win right here. If he is drawing, I am going to make him pay for it. If he was playing a 9, I want to scare him off by betting the 10. If I'm completely wrong and he is playing something like pocket queens and he calls me, I still have outs now that I have an open-end straight draw.

I easily had my opponent covered, so I decided to apply maximum pressure and bet enough to put him all-in. He called, and sure enough turned over Ac-Jc. The river brought the Js, giving him top pair but filling my straight, and I scooped a big pot. Here, I made him pay for his flush draw. He was not getting correct pot odds to chase his flush draw. If you force opponents to make those kinds of mistakes, then you will be a successful poker player. Do not worry about them drawing out on you. That will happen. In the long run, you will make money.

Let's look at another possibility with the same beginning hands above. That is, my opponent raises with Ac-Jc and I call preflop with 7s-8s. This time the flop comes Qd-9d-4s. My opponent, as his custom, automatically bets the flop after he raises preflop. I call, looking for an opportunity to take the hand on the turn. The turn brings the 2d. Again, my opponent bets. Now, I would raise here. Even if my opponent is playing a hand like A-Q, he is going to have a hard time calling with the diamond flush on board. That is the value of position. By calling on the flop, my opponent can easily put me on a flush draw. When the flush hits on the turn, I can try to steal the pot with a big raise, even though that card does not help me. In no-limit play, knowing your opponent and using position can make you a lot of money.

Now let's add another twist to the previous example. Let's take the exact same hand above, yet this time the turn brings the 2s instead of the 2d. I now have a legitimate flush draw with two spades on board. However, my bluffing potential has gone way down since I can no longer represent the diamond flush. Here, the analysis becomes more straightforward. My opponent has to feel good about his A-Q since he has top pair with top kicker. If he is smart, he will bet out, and bet enough to force me to fold any drawing hand I have. That is, he should bet enough so that I am not getting the correct pot odds to call. He should make me pay to try to draw out. If he does do that, then I fold. The only time I would not is if I believe I could win a lot of money from him on the river if I do hit my flush. This is where you have to know your opponent—especially in No Limit Hold 'Em. If he is inexperienced and will call a big bet on the river with this top pair when I make my flush, then it may be worth calling here. Up against a good player who will not pay you off, you should always fold. Now let's say my opponent does not bet out. Instead, he checks the turn here. What's my move? I check and take the free card to see if I can hit my flush. There is not a lot to be gained by betting here, and there is a lot to lose. If I bet, I invite a check-raise, in which case I cost myself money, and if he raises enough, I do not even get to see the last card.

In No Limit Hold 'Em, you have to always be careful of opening the door and inviting a raise. There are times to bluff and semi-bluff. Then there are times to take a free card. Whenever you bet or raise, you run the risk that an opponent will raise you back, and raise enough to force you out of the hand. Before you make a bet or raise, always think about what you are trying to ac-complish. Looking at the last two examples should help clarify what I am talking about. In the first example, I am willing to bluff the turn when I can represent a diamond flush. I am trying to win the pot right there. It will either work or it will not. If I get raised back, I can throw the hand away no problem. The river is not going to help me anyway. In the second example, I want to see the river. Since the board is not nearly as scary to my oppo-nent, it will be hard to chase him off the hand anyway. In this case, my goal is to see the river as cheaply as possible. A bet or raise on my part would not serve any purpose and could cost me the opportunity to make my hand if my opponent raises me.

CHAPTER NINE

The River

Okay, so you have made it to the river. All the cards are on the table. There is no more chance for improvement. There is one more round of betting to get to before you get to the showdown. What are the considerations here?

First, do you have the best hand here? If you think you have the best hand, then the goal is to maximize your profit. You want to value-bet. If you are first to act, then you should typically bet out. In no-limit play, you will want to bet the amount that you think your opponent will likely call. What that amount is will depend on the read of your opponent. An experienced opponent may actually call a bigger bet than a smaller one, since he may put

Antonio taking his first WSOP bracelet.

you on a steal with the bigger bet. The only time you would not want to bet out on the river with the best hand is if you are fairly certain your opponent will bet if you check to him. If that is the case, then go ahead and check-raise in order to extract an extra bet from your opponent.

If you are last to act with the best hand, then your only question is how much to bet or raise. Whether your opponent checks or bets, you need to bet or raise the amount that your opponent is likely to call.

Now let's look at what you should do if you are fairly certain you do not have the best hand. If you do not have the best hand, then your analysis is squarely on your opponent(s). Do you think any of them have a hand? If yes, then check and fold to any bet. If not, then you have to look at both the size of the pot and the nature of your opponents. If the pot is sizable, then it may be worth maneuvering for it. You then have to ask yourself if you can get your opponent to fold. If you are up against more than one opponent, it will be much more difficult to get everyone to fold. If you are up against a single opponent, then your read of him becomes critical. Did he miss his draw on the river? How aggressive is he? Will he fold to any sign of strength? If your opponent is the type to call down to the river any drawing hand and then fold if he misses, then by all means attack him. If he is a tough opponent who knows you will try to steal the pot and will fight back, then do not waste your money. Save those chips for a more opportune time.

The biggest decision you will ever face on the river comes when you have a hand but face a big bet from an opponent. You have a strong hand, but not the nuts, and all of a sudden you're facing an all-in bet. In fact, you were trying to figure out how to extract the most money from your opponent when he pushes in on you. What do you do? Well, before we look at some specific examples, let me emphasize an extremely important point. In no-limit play, the great majority of the time that a player makes a huge bet or raise on the river, he has the goods. If you are torn between calling and folding, it is almost always correct to fold. Remember from chapter 2 that the best way to make money is to fold. This is just as true on the river as it is preflop. You do not want to call off all of your chips with a strong but losing hand. Save those chips when you can be the one to exert the pressure. In no-limit games, you want to be the hunter, not the hunted.

Let's look at a sample hand. You're playing $10–$20 No Limit Hold 'Em and open-raise to $60 from early position with pocket queens. You get one caller, an aggressive player in late position. The flop comes Qd-Jd-3d. Bingo. You have hit top set, but the board is all diamonds. Since you do not slow-play sets (especially with all diamonds on board), you bet out $100 into the $150 pot. Your opponent calls. The turn brings a harmless 6c. With the pot now at $350, you bet out $300. Again, your opponent calls. The river brings the 9h. The pot is now $950. You bet $800 and your opponent raises all-in. It will cost you $3,400 more to call. Even though you have a strong hand, your opponent in all likelihood has a flush. Even though this opponent is aggressive, he is not stupid. If he was going to bluff, you would have expected him to make a move on the turn. This looks like a classic trap, and he may have been slow-playing the nut flush from the flop. Cut your losses, save your money, and wait for a better opportunity.

Once you see the power of making big bets or raises on the river, you can see the potential to make big bluffs as well. In no-limit play, you have the power to do that, and it can be an extremely effective move. If you are going to try this, though, a few words of caution. First, make sure you try it on the right opponent. Do not try it on a player who is going to call with any made hand. Use it against more experienced players. Do not overuse it. This is a powerful weapon that should be used sparingly if at all. The move is extremely risky. Even if you can get away with a bluff, there is always the chance that you are up against a monster hand. Finally, don't waste a significant part of your bankroll on such a move. You never want to bet (or call for that matter) an amount that will leave you crippled unless you are sure you have the winning hand.

CHAPTER TEN

Shorthanded Strategy

Shorthanded games generally have three to five players. With more than six players, you are getting close to a full table. With less than three, you are heads-up, which is the discussion of the next chapter.

When would you play shorthanded? If there is a lull at the casino at an off time like early morning or dinnertime, games will often be shorthanded. (However, with the ever-increasing popularity of poker, the lulls in cardrooms are becoming fewer and farther between.) Many online sites offer shorthanded games in which a maximum of only five or six players are allowed at a table. Many players like these tables, as they provide a faster-paced game. With fewer players, not only will you be involved in more hands, but the hands will also go quicker.

Even if you prefer to play full-table games, I would suggest that you get some shorthanded table experience. You never know when you will find yourself in a shorthanded game. The juicy game you are playing may lose a few players at an off-peak time. The only game available may be shorthanded. Or if you are playing a tournament, you will find yourself in many short-handed situations. For instance, if you are playing a nine-person single-table tournament, you are only three eliminations away from shorthanded play.

So what are the main considerations for shorthanded play? There are two big differences between shorthanded play and a full-table game. The first is your starting-hand requirements. The next is aggression. Let's talk about starting-hand requirements first.

Since you are playing shorthanded, it makes sense that you should loosen up your starting-hand requirements. That is indeed the case. The hands you would have played in middle position in a ring game now become playable in early position. However, since the texture of the game has changed, so should the texture of your starting-hand requirements. What do I mean by that? In a full-ring game, we based our starting-hand requirements on the likelihood of what our opponents could be holding and how many opponents are likely to see a flop. With fewer players, it follows that there will be fewer strong hands to contend with and that there will be fewer players seeing a flop. If that is the case, we need to adjust. Hands such as A–10 or K–J that were marginal opening hands in a full-ring game now become much stronger. Not only can these hands be played, they can be played with strength. Since these hands play best shorthanded anyway, you are better off raising with them to try to narrow the field.

Conversely, hands such as suited connectors lose some of their value in a shorthanded game. The payoff from these hands comes from flopping a monster and getting paid off from a number of opponents. In shorthanded games, you are less likely to get that much action. Why is that? In a full-ring game, when you can get to see a flop cheaply with suited connectors, you are likely to be up against three or four other opponents. When you hit a monster flop with this many opponents, there is a decent chance that at least one of them will have a playable hand and will give you some action. In a shorthanded game, when you enter a pot with your suited connectors, you may be heads-up or have two opponents at best. So even if you hit your hand, the odds are smaller that an opponent will have made something. Your chances of getting paid off are smaller.

I am not suggesting that you should not play suited connectors. What I am suggesting is that you keep this in mind and make an adjustment. If you are in a loose, passive shorthanded game with lots of preflop limpers, then play those suited connectors. If you are playing No Limit Hold 'Em and there are a couple of hyperaggressive players who are guaranteed to give you action no matter what, then you may want to play those suited connectors as well.

The next big difference in shorthanded play is aggression—or, more specifically, how aggressive you have to be. Compared to a full-ring game, you have to step it up a notch. Be more aggressive than you normally would from every position. Position is still critical, but now a hand like A-10 suited is playable from early position. Not only is it playable, you may even consider raising with it from early position. If everyone folds to you in late position, A-x suited becomes much stronger. Why would that be? Whether you are in a full-ring game or shorthanded and everyone folds to you on the button and you have A-x suited, why is that hand stronger in a shorthanded game, when in both cases you still only have the two players in the blinds to follow you? Because in a 10-handed game, there is a greater likelihood of there being better starting hands out there than in a 5-person game. If everyone folds to the button, then the chances are greater the number of players, the stronger the remaining hands are likely to be.

If there are only three players at the table, then almost any hand becomes playable if you have position. I remember playing threehanded in Colma a few years back. Phil Laak was being superaggressive, and I couldn't let him walk all over me. So I called him with the 7-2 of spades, which is far from a decent starting hand. The flop came Q-10-2 with two spades. We each get our money in the middle, which is about $6,000 each. Phil turns over the Qc-10c, making him about a 60 percent favorite. I didn't catch another spade, but the beautiful two of hearts rolled off the turn, and I got to whack the Unabomber. I don't get to whack him too often, so it was especially sweet to draw out on him.

CHAPTER ELEVEN

Heads-up Play

Heads-up play is greatly different from full-ring games or even shorthanded games. If you are just starting out, you may be wondering why you even need to know how to play heads-up. Certainly, if you are playing cash games in a casino, you are almost never likely to be playing heads-up. It is too expensive for casinos to spread such games. With the popularity of poker, it does not make sense for a cardroom to use a table and a dealer on just two players.

Having said that, I would urge every player no matter what his or her level of experience to rack up some hours playing heads-up. There are a number of reasons for doing this. First, if you play tournaments, you will eventually find yourself in a heads-up situation. Even if you are not that experienced, there are so many single-table sit-and-go tournaments offered now—both online and in casinos—that you will inevitably find yourself in a heads-up situation. Next, heads-up play is gaining in popularity. Any aspiring poker player should have a well-rounded game so that he is prepared for any new challenge. There have been many well-publicized heads-up cash games in recent years. In addition, the Golden Nugget held the first ever National Heads-Up Poker Championship featuring 64 of the best poker players in the world in a single-elimination format. I reached the final 4 in that event, and I can attribute that success to my early poker playing experience.

That brings us to the last and most critical reason for playing heads-up poker. It is a great way to gain a lot of experience in a short period of time. Whether you are just starting out or trying to get your game to the next level, playing heads-up offers you a great opportunity to improve your game. You really learn the value of hands. As we will learn shortly, you will be playing a great variety of starting hands. You will see a lot of flops, and you will learn how tough it is to make really strong hands no matter what you are holding in your hand.

When you are playing heads-up, you are totally focused on one opponent. You are forced to study his every move and mannerism. The game becomes much more about your read of your opponent than your cards. Since it will be difficult for either one of you to make hands consistently, the player who can better read his opponent will be the winner in the long run. This is tremendous practice if you aspire to be a No Limit Hold 'Em player. There is so much maneuvering and finesse in no-limit play even in a full-ring game. Heads-up play is all maneuvering and finesse. It is an ideal training ground. If you want to survive, you will quickly learn to implement more of your game than just playing your cards. If you only play your strong hands, you will not win too many hands. You will have to know when your opponent is weak and vulnerable. You will have to know what your opponent thinks of you. You will have to learn how and when to fight back when attacked. You will have to know when to push on the gas and when to throttle back. You will have to know when to trap and when to force out. You will have to know when to check, fold, and avoid traps. In short, you will have to constantly be sizing up your opponent and outmaneuvering him. Once you develop these skills, you will be a force to be reckoned with at any Hold 'Em table.

Now that we know why heads-up play is worthwhile, let's talk about some of the specific strategies relevant to heads-up play. The first thing to remember is that starting-hand requirements go out the window. Almost any hand is playable for the right price. Aggressiveness takes on added importance. Reading your opponent is critical. The one constant between heads-up play and full-ring games is that position is still paramount.

In a full-table game, the best way to make money is to fold. Inexperienced players tend to play way too many hands. When you are heads-up, though, folding is the best way to go broke. If you have the button, you should almost never fold preflop. Since you are going to have position throughout the postflop betting rounds, you do not want to surrender that advantage easily. Think of heads-up play like a tennis match. When you have position, you want to hold serve. If you can consistently hold serve and break your opponent's serve periodically, you will do fine. You want to be aggressive when you have position, but not stupid. Your primary focus should be on your opponent. You need to know how strong or weak he is in order to play properly. If he is weak, you can be aggressive no matter what you are holding. In fact, I would suggest that you do bet aggressively no matter what you are holding in that situation. If you consistently do this, it will make it very difficult for your opponent to know what you have. If you think he is strong, then you have to slow down in order to avoid being trapped.

When you are playing heads-up, any pair is a strong hand. If you flop bottom pair, don't think, "Oh no," but rather "How sweet." It's hard to make a pair, and you probably have the best hand. Let me give you an example of how powerful a pair can be. I was playing in a $20–$40 heads-up no-limit game. My opponent had about $12K in front of him, and I had him covered. I was on the button with 5-7 of hearts and raised to $140. He called. The flop came 2-5-8 with two spades. He bet $250. What should I do here? Folding was not even an option with middle pair in this situation. So my choices were to call or raise. What would raising accomplish here? Well, maybe he was on a stone-cold bluff with a hand like Q-J, and I could prevent him from drawing out on me. What if he had two spades, though? He was certainly not going to fold a flush draw because our stacks are too big. So I did not want to make the pot any bigger with second pair if he's on a flush draw. Plus, what if he reraised? I would probably have to give up on the pot. I really could not see any value in raising in this situation. Now if I had nothing, it might be correct to raise, but since I had something, I thought it was just as correct to call. So I did.

The turn peeled off the 10h. He fired $900 at the pot right away. Then it was time for the think tank. What hand could he have there? If he really had the top pair he tried to represent on the flop, why would he bet so much on the turn? Shouldn't the overcard scare him a little bit? So I thought that took his having an 8 in his hand out of the question. Could he have hit the 10? Maybe he bluffed at the pot with J-10 and got there? Maybe he flopped a set? Most people have a tendency to check when they flop a set, so I took that out of the equation. In the final analysis, I thought it was most likely he was on a draw with a slight chance that he hit the 10.

Knowing that, what was my move here? Even though I was fairly certain he was on a draw, was there any value in raising? What if I raised and he moved in on me? Did I really want to call off a monster pot with third pair? What if he is stone-cold bluffing? Do I want to shut him down and prevent him from firing at me again on the river? Again, I think the right play here was just calling. If he was on a draw and got there, well, that's poker, and sometimes that is just the way it has to go down. If he did not get there, then the advantages to me were huge, and I thought that more than made up for the fact that I was letting him draw.

Let's dig a little deeper into the theory of this hand. If he had a hand like 6s-7s and I raised him, he could very well have moved in on me, or at a minimum called to see the river, considering he had a ton of outs. The last thing I wanted to do is open the door for him to move in on me and prevent me from seeing the hand to the river. This is a critical difference between limit and no-limit play. There will be times in no-limit play when you are sure you have the best hand, yet you do not want to raise and allow your opponent to reraise and shut you out. Now what if I had raised here and was wrong in my read and my opponent really had a set, but I was so sure in my read that he had a draw that I called that all-in bet. I would have been drawing dead. Yet if I just called the turn and the river, I would have saved myself $8k. So, all things considered, I called the turn bet.

The river brought the Qd. The final board was 2-5-8-10-Q, with no flush on board. There was an outside chance at a straight if he was playing J-9. My opponent bet out $2,500. Once again, I visited the think tank. He definitely did not have the 8 he represented on the flop, because he clearly would not bet that much with third pair. I was also fairly certain that he did not have the 10, because again I did not think he would bet that much with an overcard now on board. So what were his likely hands? He either flopped a set, made some kind of funky two pair, hit a queen on the river, or was on some sort of draw. Of all of those, I still felt most confident that he was on a draw and missed. I decided to go with my gut and called the bet with fourth pair. I still thought my fives were good. "Good call," he said. I never did see his hand, but obviously he was drawing to a straight or a flush and missed. By calling on the turn rather than raising, I gave him another opportunity to bluff at the pot instead of risking the possible reraise on the turn.

Remember that in heads-up play, any pair is huge. You want to play every hand if you can. Put your opponent on the defensive. Always keep him guessing and never give up. Fire, fire, fire. Keep firing at him, and you'll force him to take a stand when you have a strong hand. Build it and take it. Build it before the flop and take it after the flop. Remember, making a hand is hard.

So now that we know why and how you should play heads-up, where can you get heads-up experience? As I mentioned before, brick-and-mortar cardrooms are not going to offer heads-up cash games. Most online sites, however, will offer heads-up games ranging in price from play money to very high blinds. Anyone can find a game to suit his or her price range. However, playing online does limit your ability to read your opponents, which is one of the critical reasons for playing heads up. I would suggest that you arrange as many heads-up matches with poker-playing buddies as you can. These do not have to be expensive matches.

Be creative. Play for things other than money. When I was just starting out, I would play my roommates to see who would take out the garbage or do the dishes or vacuum the apartment or any other chore that needed to be done. With just that much at stake, we would play for hours on end in real grudge matches, fighting for every chip. Try it, and I guarantee you will never regret it.

Always remember that the strategies and starting-hand requirements for heads-up play are greatly different from a full-table game. Learn what you can from heads-up play, but do not forget to switch gears when you head back to a full-table game.

CHAPTER TWELVE

Table Image

There are essentially two distinct table images. First, there is the image of the wild and crazy guy. This is an extremely tough image to pull off. You want to appear to be playing fast and loose so that you will get action when you hit a hand. The thing is that in order to appear fast and loose, you have to play a lot of hands even when you are out of position.

In order to be the crazy guy, you have to be aggressive, and you have to be comfortable playing that style. Not only do you have to open up your starting requirements, you have to play marginal hands with strength. This is not an easy feat to pull off. The rewards for such an image can be huge for the rare player

WORLDWIDE POKER NEWS   POKER STRATEGIES FROM THE PROS   ONLINE POKER ACTION

THE POKER AUTHORITY

Card Player

Antonio Esfandiari
Performs Poker Wizardry
at L.A. Poker Classic

www.CardPlayer.com

PLUS   Exploiting Tilt
Pot Odds Made Easy
Political Attitudes of Players

Vol. 17/No. 7   March 26, 2004

Antonio on the cover of *Card Player*.

who can successfully employ it. When you make a hand with a marginal holding, you are likely to get paid off because your hand will be well hidden and your opponents will be justifiably cynical. The key to pulling off this style is knowing when to slow down if need be. If you are playing with weak tight players, it can be very effective—although when a player does fight back, he probably has something. If you are playing against some strong aggressive players, this type of style can get very expensive very quickly. You cannot keep betting marginal hands, yet you cannot let these aggressive types always chase you away when you do.

I highly recommend that all beginning or inexperienced players start off playing the second type of style. This is the tight conservative style. That is, you generally stick with the starting-hand requirements outlined earlier. You play basic fundamental poker with a slight twist. You use your conservative image to periodically steal pots. Now, I am not talking about blind stealing or positional raises. Those strategies should be part of your basic arsenal. I am talking about occasionally making a stone-cold bluff into a big pot when you sense your opponent is weak. For example, say you call from late position with 7-8 suited. The flop comes 5-5-2 with none in your suit. Even though you have nothing, you know this flop didn't help your opponent, either, so you call a bet on the flop. If the turn brings another blank, you can make a play for the pot. Regardless of whether your opponent checks or bets, make a play at him. Unless your opponent has a strong hand, he cannot call you. Your conservative image has bought you some equity.

Keep in mind, though, that you do not want to make those strategic bluffs against an opponent who is not smart enough to be paying attention to your conservative play. Also, you want to make sure not to try such moves in multiway pots in which the likelihood of someone holding a real hand is greater.

As you gain more experience, your ultimate goal should be to mix up your play. This will serve two purposes. First, it will keep your opponents off balance and guessing which are always more profitable for you. Next, as you become more comfortable shifting gears, you can adapt to your opponents' varying styles. If you sit down to a tight table and start out aggressively, and then you notice that everyone else is starting to loosen up, you may want to tighten up a little bit. There is one phenomenon that is pretty consistent in poker. When a new table starts, the play tends to be conservative. This is the result of a combination of things. Players want to take their time getting accustomed to the game. Players want to size one another up. Some players have promised themselves that they are going to play tight, conservative poker and not go on tilt. And nobody is stuck any money yet. After a few times around the table and a couple of pots build, though, you will usually find that the table loosens up considerably.

That is just one example of the changing dynamics of a table. You should, of course, always be focused on the texture of the game. You should also know each opponent's tendencies and how the players react to one another. A fairly tight game can loosen up considerably with the addition of one loose player.

If you are going to play No Limit Hold 'Em, there are two factors that become so much more important than they are in limit play. These are table image and reading your opponent. In limit play, you can win money by playing fundamentally sound poker. That is, stick to solid hands and play them strongly. Play your cards and make correct decisions and you can grind out wins. That is not enough in no-limit play, however. The stakes are just too high. If someone is going to make a pot-sized bet or an all-in reraise, you have to know something about your opponent. If you are going to make a big bet or raise yourself, you have to know how your opponents will react. If you are making a bet to push someone off the pot, you better be sure that your table image will back you up.

No Limit Hold 'Em is a very artful game. Limit Hold 'Em is more of a math game. There is more mental warfare going on in no-limit play. I would suggest that you try to experiment at some lower levels. Start out with a smaller buy-in so you are not afraid to risk too much. Change up your styles, and take notice of how your opponents are reacting. Pay attention to everything going on. Watch the styles of everyone else at the table, and see how the other players are reacting to different styles. If you stay focused on everything and experiment with different styles, you will soon find yourself being able to seamlessly switch gears and play at optimal strategy for the table.

Poker takes a lot of practice. No Limit Hold 'Em is a game that takes 10 minutes to learn but a lifetime to master. Once you have the fundamentals of Hold 'Em down, you still have a lot of work to do. You will need to do a lot of experimenting in order to find a comfort zone. You want the game to open up for you so you can see everything clearly. In order to accomplish that, you must be able to maneuver and manipulate your opponents. That can only happen with the right table image. Like any other aspect of your game, your table image will take lots of hours of hard work and practice.

When I was practicing magic 12 hours a day every day, I was not just focusing on the tricks. Well, at first I was. Once I got the fundamentals down, though, I knew I had to work on my performance. I had to be able to make the tricks appear effortless. Becoming a successful magician was going to take more than just the ability to perform some tricks. I was going to have to be a showman. My image was paramount to my success.

When I started playing poker, it was the same thing. At first, I concentrated on learning the fundamentals. If I was going to take my game to the next level, I knew I would have to work on my image. Your opponents are your audience. Play to them. Make your tricks appear effortless.

I like to befriend everyone at the table. If I can loosen them up, they are likely to let their guard down. I ask a player a question, and he might give away his hand. Poker is a boring sport at times. I like to keep it going at the table. Whenever someone makes a big bet at me, I like to ask him what he has. He starts counting his chips, and then I say, "No, what are your cards?" That usually gets a chuckle, followed by a response of some type. What he doesn't realize is that his response in some way or another gives away information about his hand.

CHAPTER THIRTEEN

The Texture of the Game

When we refer to the texture of the game, we are talking about the overall play of the table based on the collective composition of each of the individual players seated there. While every game is unique, many players have similar styles, and the play at a table can often be categorized into specific types. Before we take a look at these types, however, keep in mind that these are just generalizations. The texture of a game is fluid. That is, it is constantly evolving and changing. Some of your opponents will change their play in midstream. A player who loses a big pot may go on tilt or he may tighten up, depending on his nature. Players will come and go from the table. The introduction of one maniac to a previously tight table can drastically alter the texture of the game. If you are playing online, the turnover at your table is likely to be high, so you need to pay particularly close attention. If the overall play at a table is loose aggressive, there still may be a couple of solid, tight aggressive players there. The bottom line is that no matter where you are playing or who you are playing against, you will need to stay focused on both the texture of the game and the play of each opponent individually. Winning players consistently make the necessary adjustments. Losing players do not. With that in mind, let's take a look at some of the different styles of play.

LOOSE AGGRESSIVE PLAY

These are players who like action. They will call or even raise with marginal hands regardless of their position. Put a couple of these players at the same table and watch the chips fly. There will be a steady stream of raises and reraises preflop, which will not deter any of these players from seeing a flop. You will mostly find these kinds of tables at the lower limits where a lot of inexperienced players like to frequent. Invariably, a number of these players will be more interested in splashing their chips around than in making a profit. There are, surprisingly, also a lot of higher-stakes tables that can be categorized as loose aggressive. So no matter what your level of experience, you are going to need to know how to play in these games.

First and foremost, resist the temptation to join in the party. Loose aggressive play can pay great dividends in the short run, but in the long run it is a losing proposition. When playing in a game dominated by these players, you have to be more selective in your starting-hand requirements. Drawing hands lose their attractiveness because it will be hard to draw for the right price. If you know you are likely facing a number of raises and reraises, you do not want to get sucked into a pot. Even if you think you can see a flop relatively cheaply, a good flop for you could get very expensive. For instance, say you are holding 6-5 suited in the cutoff position. By the time the action gets to you, it will "only" cost you three times the amount of the big blind to call. Since that is cheap for this game, you are tempted to call and in fact do call. Now that flop comes 9-7-4 with one of your suit. On its face, this does not appear to be a bad flop for you. You have an open-end straight draw and a back-door flush draw. A closer examination, however, would reveal just how dangerous this flop is for you in a game like this.

First off, right now you have nothing. Even though you have a draw, you are most likely facing an expensive one given the texture of this game. Next, if you do catch an 8 to complete your draw, you run the risk that an opponent holding J-10 will make a bigger straight. So even though this flop is not a bad one for 6-5 suited, it might not be worth playing, because it might cost you a big part of your stack to see the turn. It is not worth semi-bluffing here, since you are likely to get called or even raised by these players. In fact, bluffing hardly ever works in a loose aggressive game. Rather, you should be looking to value-bet strong hands.

In a loose aggressive game, you are better off waiting for big hands, such as middle to top pairs or big cards. For instance, say you play K-Q suited and the flop comes 9-7-4 with two of your suit. Now you are in better shape to play after the flop. You have two overcards and a flush draw. If you hit anything, you may have the best hand in this loose game.

In a loose aggressive game, you should not be trying to trap opponents with hands like small suited connectors or little pairs. Furthermore, you should not attempt to hide the value of your big hands. Since you are likely to get action, play good hands and bet them for value while folding your smaller drawing hands.

In a loose aggressive game, you are likely to face greater fluctuations in your chip stack because the pots will be bigger on average. If that discourages you, find a tighter game. If it is not a deterrent, keep in mind that you only need to win a few of those big pots to have a winning session, as long as you consistently avoid the temptation to play those marginal and weak hands.

Finally, when up against loose aggressive players, try to get position on them. If there is one maniac at the table and a seat opens up to his left, switch seats. You want players like that on your right.

LOOSE PASSIVE PLAY

The weakest players are loose passive. They play almost any hand but never play aggressively. They are essentially relying on the luck of the cards to win out for them. What happens is that they will end up calling a lot of bets when they are beat, and they will fail to get the maximum amount of money when they have a strong hand. As you can imagine, this does not make for a profitable poker session, especially when there are a few experienced players at the table waiting to take advantage.

How should you play at a loose aggressive table in order to take maximum advantage? In this environment, drawing hands go up in value. Those small suited connectors like 6-5 are more valuable because you can usually try to draw out other players rather inexpensively. Conversely, bigger hands lose some of their value. This does not mean that you should throw pocket aces away preflop. Rather, you should try to narrow the field as much as possible. If you play aces preflop against four other opponents

and the flop comes something like Q-10-8 (with two hearts),
you are probably in trouble.

In a no-limit game, you can work the action both ways. If
you have a drawing hand, limp in and see a flop cheaply against a
number of opponents. If you have a big pair, raise big to get the
flop heads-up. In a limit game, it will be much more difficult to
chase out the loose passive players with your one raise. You
should still play your big hands in limit action, but be prepared to
dump them if you do not like the flop. One pair is unlikely to
hold up against four opponents.

Similar to the loose aggressive game, bluffing is not likely
to work here. There is an old saying in poker that you can't bluff
a sucker. If players are going to call you down with anything,
then wait until you have a winning hand and let them call you
down.

TIGHT PASSIVE PLAY

A tight passive player is someone who will only play strong hands
but will not play with any aggression. These are ideal opponents
in that they are easy to read. If they have a hand, you will know it
because they will fold otherwise. Since the great majority of the
time they will not have a hand, you will be able to chase them out
and scoop the pot. Against these types of players, your goal is to
win a lot of small pots and avoid losing any big ones. If they're
calling you, they have a hand.

Aggressive play and bluffing will pay off for you against this
type of play. When you are aggressive against a tight passive opponent, one of two things will happen. If he does not have a
hand, you will chase him out and scoop up the pot. If he does
have a hand, he will call (and possibly even raise), in which case
you have gained some valuable information. You now know that

he has a hand and you should put on the brakes if you do not have a strong hand.

TIGHT AGGRESSIVE PLAY

Tight aggressive players make tough opponents. They are not interested in splashing chips around for the sake of doing it. They will not call you down with anything. They will not waste chips chasing draws when they are not getting sufficient odds to do so. If they do enter a pot, they will not give up easily. They will play aggressively until they think that they are beat. They will implement strategic bluffs and will try to trap you when they can. In short, these types of players are the furthest thing from dead money.

When faced with these types of players, you can do one of two things. First, you can look for a more profitable table, which may be a good idea if you cannot beat the game. Next, you can try to beat them. Since you are likely to face at least a couple of these players at most tables, let's look at how to play against them.

Not all tight aggressive players are created equally. Some will play strictly by the book. That is, they will only enter a pot when they have the goods, and they will get out if their hand does not improve and faces some competition. If they do have a hand, they will play it aggressively, betting and raising (or even check-raising) at every opportunity. Even though these players are playing solid, they are easy to read and can be beat.

Other tight aggressive players will be more creative. They will use position as well as their cards to play aggressively. They will not easily give up on a hand, especially if they think that their opponent may be weak. They will not be afraid to bluff and semi-bluff or reraise when they think they are being bluffed.

These players will be your toughest opponents and will require a great deal of your focus. If you can't figure out their play, don't guess. There is no shame in being bluffed out of a pot. Remember that you will make money by folding when you are beat. Good players know that, and that is why good players can be bluffed. So long as you stay focused against these opponents, you will begin to pick up a lot about their play, and you will know when to attack and when to retreat.

HYBRID TABLES

While a lot of poker tables will have a distinctive feel (that is, the play at the table is generally loose aggressive), most cannot be easily categorized. More likely, you will be facing a number of different styles of play at the same table. There will be a mix of tight aggressive, tight passive, loose aggressive, and loose passive players sitting around you. Additionally, there may be a couple of rather advanced players who will continuously mix up their play and will be hard to pigeonhole to a particular type.

While it is extremely helpful to size up your opponents as a particular type, keep in mind that a poker game is fluid. A loose aggressive player may tighten up if he takes a bad beat or may go completely on tilt. Another player may sit down with all good intentions of playing tight aggressive, and in fact he starts out that way. After a few rounds of play in which he has not played a hand, he may go back to old habits and loosen up significantly. Your goal as a poker player is to determine how each of your opponents is playing at the moment and adapt accordingly. You must adjust to each player, and often you will be facing different types of players in the same hand. Recognize that and use it to your advantage.

For example, let's say you see a flop in early position with pocket queens. The flop comes 10-9-4 with two hearts. There are two players behind you. The first is loose aggressive and the second is loose passive. You think you have the best hand at the moment but would like to narrow the field since there are both straight and flush draws on the board. However, both your opponents are loose, so how do you chase them out? Fortunately, the loose aggressive player will act right behind you. If you bet, you know he is likely to raise. While the loose passive player is likely to call one bet, there is a good chance that he will fold to a bet and a raise. So go ahead and bet out, knowing the loose aggressive player will raise, which will help chase out the loose passive player.

Knowing each player's tendencies will help you exploit opportunities. I remember playing in a game with a friend of mine named Marcus who was loose aggressive. I had position on him and was just looking for an opportunity to take him when the following hand came up. A guy named Kevin opened in second position for $100 with pocket queens. About six players called, including Marcus. I was sitting on the button with 9–10. Since I had position and there were so many players in the pot, I called. The flop came 5-8-J. I had an open-end straight draw. Kevin still had an overpair. He checked his queens, and some other guy bet $500. Marcus called as did I. Kevin then check-raised to $2500. Everyone now folded to Marcus, who called. The bet was now $2,000 more to me. I had about $7,000 in front of me. Both Marcus and Kevin had me covered, but not by much.

At this point, I knew that Kevin had me beat. I also knew Kevin was a tight aggressive player who can lay down a hand. I also knew Marcus is loose aggressive and could be playing anything. I moved all-in. I was fairly confident that Kevin would fold, and I hoped Marcus would fold as well. Even if they didn't, I still had a number of outs to make my straight. Remember, I couldn't see their cards, so from my perspective I had eight outs (four 7s and four Qs).

Kevin thought forever and finally folded his hand. Marcus called instantly. We did not turn over our cards. The turn and the river were a two and a three. There was about $17,000 in the pot, and neither one of us wanted to show his cards. Marcus was first to act, though, and he said, "I missed." I said, "Me, too." He turned over his 6–7 for a 7 high, and I took home the pot with a 10 high. The only reason I won that pot is because I understood the texture of the game and the nature of each player. When Marcus only called Kevin's check-raise bet, I knew Marcus was on a draw. If he had made a hand, he would have reraised Kevin. In my thought process, I thought I could get him off his drawing hand with a big-enough raise. If I had any less money, I don't even try this move. However, a lot of good things could have happened here. First, they both could have folded, and I would have won a sizable pot. Next, one or both of them could have called me, and I could have drawn out and won a huge pot. Finally, I might have been called and lost my stack. Even in this third scenario, think how great it was for my table image when everyone saw me putting all that money in with a draw. I was likely to get plenty of action in later pots when I had a hand. As it turned out, I won the pot and everyone got to see me going all-in on a draw.

STAY AHEAD OF THE GAME

Just as you are trying to get inside your opponents' heads, they will be (or should be anyway) trying to get inside yours. Don't be predictable. Always be aware of what your opponents think of your play. The table image you think you may have may not match up with what your opponents think of you. Different opponents may think differently of you. Stay ahead of the game. If players think you are tight, then use that to steal from them. If you get caught, so be it. Instead of worrying that your opponents are on to you, value-bet hands knowing that your opponents may now call, thinking that you are trying to steal.

If you stay focused on the texture of the game and consistently adjust as the texture adjusts, you should do just fine in the long run. However, you are not going to beat every game. Poker is a streaky game, and every player will have losing sessions. Be objective in determining why you are losing. If you are truly experiencing bad luck and have a good read on your opponents, then hang in there for a while longer. In the long run, luck evens out and skill triumphs. If, however, you are losing because you are being outplayed, then it may be time to leave. Are other players anxious to challenge you? Are all of your bluff attempts met with resistance? Do players play more aggressively against you than they do against others? Be honest in answering these questions.

Remember that the best way to make money is to fold. Well, there is a corollary to that rule. If you are getting beat, get up. Notice that I did not say that if you are losing, get up. There is a subtle but big difference. If you are losing but feel that you are playing well and can beat the game, then stay with it. On the other hand, if you are losing because you are getting beat, then get up. Find another table or take a break. Too often, players compound their mistakes by sticking with a losing situation. They do not want to leave the table until they get their money back. If you are losing because you are getting beat, then the longer you play, the more you will lose. Conversely, players make a similar mistake when they are winning. They make a nice gain and want to quit while they are ahead. If you are ahead because you are outplaying your opponents, then you should stick with the game unless you are starting to tire out. You have favorable equity in this game.

Your table image is apt to be favorable, and your opponents probably fear you. That is a situation you want to keep exploiting.

When choosing a game, the texture is an important consideration. Know your own style and what game suits you best. Personally, I like to be the aggressor at the table. I don't want to play at a table full of overly aggressive players because that neutralizes my strength. Find a game that feeds your strengths.

CHAPTER FOURTEEN

Playing Online

The Internet offers players a great way to gain experience in a hurry. Playing online can also help you work on certain aspects of the game. Poker is both an art and a science. Even though No Limit Texas Hold 'Em is more artful than Limit Hold 'Em, there is still a science to it. When you are playing with live players, there is so much feel to the game that it is easy for some players to ignore the science aspect. I find playing online is a great way to work on that part of your game. So whether you are a neophyte or a seasoned pro, online play has something to offer. With so many players logged on at any given time, you will have no problem finding a table that suits your needs. If you're looking for me, you can usually find me at the "MagicAntonio" table at Ultimatebet.com. Before you plug in, though, let's go over some finer points of playing on the Net.

BONE UP ON YOUR MATH

Online poker is more game theory than anything else. Math is all important, and patience is a virtue. Since you cannot get a true tell from your opponents, you will have to play more conservatively. Rely on quality starting hands and play in a more straight-up style. It is more difficult to simply outplay opponents when you cannot look them in the eye. Just because you cannot see them, though, does not mean that you cannot get a read on your opponents. The biggest tell in any game (brick and mortar or online) is betting patterns. Concentrate on how your opponent bets certain hands in different situations. Get your reads that way, stick with quality hands, and know what kind of pot odds you are getting. Concentrate on the fundamentals to make them as solid as can be. Then, when you step into a live cardroom, you will have a solid foundation to build on.

POSITION IS EVERYTHING

As we already have learned, Texas Hold 'Em is a positional game. If you have position, you have a great advantage. Position is even bigger on the Net because it is the only real edge you have. Never forget that. All you have is position. I try to play only when I have position.

DON'T GO ON TILT

When you play in a brick-and-mortar casino, you have to physically pick up your chips and commit them to the pot. You see them, touch them, and release them. You have a real sense that you are putting cold hard cash in the pot. When you are playing online, you click on a mouse to commit some cyberchips. Those chips are no less real than the ones you have in a casino. Remember that. You must not play hands that you know you shouldn't.

Online play is so much faster than a brick-and-mortar game because each deal is automatic. There is no need to shuffle, because the computer program can generate a random deck instantly. So you are going to see a lot more hands in an hour's time. That means more good hands, more bad hands, more suck-outs, and more bad beats. Even some very experienced players can get frustrated and go on tilt. Combine this with the ease of committing your chips via a mouse click and things can get ugly in a hurry. Keep this in mind: stay patient and remain disciplined.

STAY FOCUSED

Even though online play is much quicker than a live game, it tends to be more boring. There is no visual stimulus. You cannot observe all of the various idiosyncrasies of your opponents. Now, add to that the fact that you are playing in the comfort of your home with a multitude of distractions, and you can see that it is very easy to lose focus. If you're watching the basketball game on TV while talking on the phone and playing with the kids, it's going to be tough to concentrate on the poker table on your computer screen.

When you play online, give it the same attention and focus you would a live game. Avoid multitasking. Many Internet players play more than one table at a time. If you're just starting out, I would recommend against that. However, once you gain experience, you can try playing more tables as long as it does not affect your overall focus. Most sites allow you to preselect your move before the action gets to you, which makes it easier to juggle multiple tables. I would caution against doing this, though, be-cause you are giving off a tell. For example, if you mark the check/fold button when you miss the flop and the action is checked to you, it will be obvious to the other players that you selected that button when you checked quickly in turn. When the turn card helps you and you bet, your opponents are going to know that you had nothing after the flop, because you were will-ing to fold.

Take Good Notes

It is very easy to go on autopilot and just focus on your cards and not pay attention to what is going on in the hands you are not in-volved in. One way to avoid this is to take notes. In fact, note-keeping is huge in Internet play. Since you are not going to remember someone's face, you have to keep meticulous records of your opponents. Get yourself a logbook and keep track of all of the other players. This is a must.

If you typically play on the same site at the same limits around the same time of day, you are sure to face a lot of the same opponents over and over again. Take good notes on each player's betting patterns and styles. You will find this information invalu-able. I know some very successful online players who have great big logbooks of their opponents.

One handy tool available on most sites is the ability to re-trieve hand histories. You can get these for any hand you were dealt cards, even if you folded them. And for any hand played to the river, you will find out the cards played by each player who lasted to the showdown, even if that player mucked his cards. For example, say you fold preflop and then witness a very interesting hand between two opponents. The hand goes to a showdown. The winning player is called. Once his hand is revealed, the losing player mucks his cards. You can retrieve the hand history to find out what the losing player had.

Hand histories are also great for analyzing your own play. In the heat of the moment, it is hard to take notes or to remember every bet made. So take advantage of hand histories, take good notes, and make yourself an Internet winner.

The Magician, The Unabomber, and The Guy Who Never Wins

by Rob Fulop

I've come down to Vegas from San Francisco to pay a four-day visit to my pals Antonio Esfandiari and Phil "Unabomber" Laak. I used to hang out with both of them last year, back when they were both still poker mortals, back when our $10–$20 twice weekly No Limit Hold 'Em game in San Francisco felt like the Big Game. Less than two years ago, I loaned Antonio a few thousand so that he could buy into his first ever WPT event, the "Gold Rush." After his spectacular TV performance, his first ever, where he tortured Phil Hellmuth, well . . . things just got better and better for Kid 44 (Antonio's nickname, the "44" comes from the fact that he won $44K for his third place Gold Rush finish). Since then, he has won first place at the Commerce WPT event last year, and a WSOP bracelet for Pot Limit Hold 'Em, netting over $1.5 million in prize money.

It's 1:30 p.m. on a Saturday afternoon in Las Vegas.

Antonio is sitting on the couch in the living room of his new house, courtesy of the World Poker Tour. He is wearing only his boxers; in one hand is a bottle of apple juice, in the other, a computer mouse. Antonio has been awake for less than 15 minutes and he's already playing high stakes online poker. Looking up from the laptop precariously perched on his knee, his hung-over eyes light up to greet me as he flashes me his patented "good to see you" smile.

"Doctor Philips, how can I be so lucky to have you visit me!" Antonio has been intentionally mispronouncing my name ever since we met a few years ago. But as annoying as it is to constantly be referred to by the wrong last name, I just can't help but feel welcome.

One part Aladdin, one part Bugs Bunny, Antonio is a likable, but somewhat annoying, tall, dark, and handsome Persian wise-guy. He has a natural ability to make anybody and everybody feel like his best friend in the world. Even though you know he's feeding you a crock of B.S., you just don't care. That's how charming he is. He's slick, somewhat cocky, yet at the same time, undeniably likable.

Antonio's warm greeting is quickly interrupted by the onscreen action. His head jerks back to the laptop . . . studying intently . . . both eyes focused on the screen. He calls out to the other two guys in the room, both of whom are deeply immersed in their own online poker games.

"Hey guys . . . what should I do with this? Gawd, Please let me felt SPIRIT ROCK today . . . just one time!"

I look over Antonio's shoulder. Sure enough, "KID44" is playing in a three-handed $25–$50 game with "SPIRIT ROCK," who is arguably the best online No Limit poker player in the world. Seconds earlier, Antonio had called Spirit's $150 button raise from the middle blind, holding 6♠ 5♠? He checked the flop consisting of 2-4-Q with two spades, and is contemplating what to do about Spirit's $350 bet. Phil and Dave, put down their laptops and join me to gather around Antonio's laptop, immediately discussing whether Antonio should go all in for $3,125, his entire stack, or just call SPIRIT ROCK's $350 flop bet.

"Call!" suggests Dave, a seasoned online pro, and the more conservative of the bunch. "If you miss, you could always pick up the pot anyway. Spirit probably doesn't have anything—he usually doesn't."

Phil Laak stares at the screen, stuffing the remains of a half eaten jelly donut into his mouth that had been sitting on the coffee table for two days. Phil comes across as a total goofball upon first meeting him: the stained sweatshirt, the nerdy glasses, the unmatched socks. Phil has the "screw is loose" act down to a fine art. But unlike Antonio, who is very much a "what you see is what you get" kinda guy, Phil has three different levels going on at the same time. On the surface is the wacky goofball he wants you to think that he is: unorganized, disheveled; if Gilligan played poker, he'd be Phil. But even after a short while you get the sense that there really is a method to his meticulously crafted madness, that underneath the unwashed hair lies a brain which is constantly in high gear, maybe even some sort of genius. But then if you get to know Phil even better, well, what you realize is that, actually, at his deepest level, Phil is basically just a goofball after all.

As fragments of jelly donut spew from his mouth, the Unabomber offers his analysis, disagreeing loudly with Dave's prudent suggestion.

"DUDE! How can you flat CALL? Your draw is too BIG! Put his butt ALL IN and punish him. What could he have anyway? How can he call? And if he does call . . . well . . . then just get there. You're almost even money against an over-pair."

Antonio's mind is racing furiously, trying to decide what to do with his big draw, but still he can't help wasting five of his remaining ten seconds to fling a backhanded insult to Phil.

"Look Phil, I'm not the luck-box that you are. I don't just get there on demand like you."

At this point, Phil is wiping grape jelly off of his mouth with his hands and smearing them onto his boxers, trying to ignore Antonio's insult to his poker prowess.

Five seconds left to decide. Call or raise? Tick . . . tick . . . tick . . .

Since I'm the Guy Who Never Wins, my advice is neither offered, nor solicited. Six months prior, I was the guy who could terrorize any No Limit Hold 'Em game I sat down in. But that was then, and now is now. Fifteen consecutive "all-in" bad beats and a long string of unflopped sets later, I'm now the Guy Who Never Wins. Frankly, I'm asking (1) Why in the world Antonio is going up against

Spirit Rock in the first place; I mean, surely there are 'softer spots' available. (2) Why did he call a button raise out of position holding a six high?

With a soft sigh, Antonio slides the BET bar to the far right, and clicks the BET button, betting every last dollar of his $3,125 stack. Now it's Spirit Rock's turn to think. The seconds tick by like hours. Nobody utters a sound, the four of us transfixed on the screen. Antonio breaks the silence by asking nobody in particular, "Will I ever win again?" Three seconds later, Spirit folds and the pot is unceremoniously shoved toward Antonio's online chair. Phil and Dave return to their own games, back to business as usual.

I do a quick scan of Antonio's new house: wall-to-wall white carpets flank bare white walls; not a plant or picture in sight. The oversized flat screen television dominates the living room, along with a few dozen DVDs—a classic male film collection, consisting of the better crime, action adventure, and, obviously, poker related films. Bellagio chips, ranging from $10 to $1,000, lie scattered over the coffee table, serving as drink coasters. A rubber-banded two-inch thick wad of $100 bills sitting on one of the cushions of the sofa looks as if somebody just tossed it there a few days ago and forgot about it. I'm in poker dreamland.

I walk into the kitchen, brushing past the two half-empty boxes of leftover Chinese food sitting on the kitchen countertop, along with the remains of last night's outdoor barbecue. Every plate and piece of silverware in the house is piled up in the sink, waiting to be washed. A high-end liquor collection sits on the counter facing outwards toward the pool and hot tub, many of the bottles half empty (or half full, depending on how you happen to be running that day). Obviously, in this house the fun never ends.

A few hours later, I'm ready to go play poker. I'm going to start out small; perhaps the $3-$5 No Limit game at the Sands. Dave is still playing online poker. Antonio is returning phone calls to assorted friends, his agent, and various poker publicists. As much fun as it is to hang out with Antonio, I sometimes get the feeling that I'm being squeezed in between telephone conversations.

I'm planning to drop Phil off at the Bellagio, where he left his car a few nights ago. His '68 Cadillac Coupe DeVille (customized convertible, roof cut off)

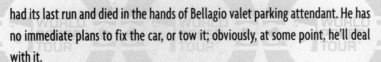

had its last run and died in the hands of Bellagio valet parking attendant. He has no immediate plans to fix the car, or tow it; obviously, at some point, he'll deal with it.

As we are putting on our shoes, Phil notices an opened package inside the door. It's a complimentary overnight bag bearing the logo of Light, the nightclub at the Bellagio. Antonio and his "Rocks n' Rings" posse are regulars at this exclusive venue. Whenever they show up, however long the line, they receive VIP treatment, breezing past the hordes waiting to ascend the escalator, and escorted to a velvet roped "reserved" table. Phil can't help but take advantage of the opportunity to tease Antonio about the bag. "Hey Rob, check it OUT. If you spend $100,000 at Light, they give you this cool bag!"

Later the following evening, the four of us head out to the Mandalay Bay for dinner. The conversation starts off with the requisite poker war stories, consisting of bad beats and busted bankrolls. Three bottles of wine later, after a spirited disagreement about which strip club in Las Vegas is hands down the best one, we move on to complexities of the human heart. We gossip about another friend of ours, a successful player, who recently started seeing a female dealer and is now moving in. It's common for poker players to sprinkle poker jargon into such conversations. A woman who is pressuring for a commitment is bluffing. If somebody is not seeing anybody at the time they are currently on the rail, the term for sitting out of the poker action.

The tradition in this group is to always gamble for the check. Typically, Antonio pulls out some cards from his pocket, which he shuffles under the table, and we each pick one. Whoever draws the lowest card picks up the tab. Having lost this gamble the last few times I was lured into playing, I refuse to participate. But they won't hear of it; the $100 bill that I toss onto the table representing my share of the dinner tab is stuffed back into my shirt pocket. They insist that I gamble for the check.

"Okay. If I can be the guy shuffling the cards, I'll play," I say.

My request to take on the role of card shuffler is met with stunned silence by my dinner companions because, even though Antonio is a semi-professional magician and expert card "mechanic," for some reason, he is always the designated shuffler of the cards.

"But Rob, Antonio always shuffles the cards."

"I don't care. If you want me to play, those are my conditions!"

With a shrug, Antonio picks out three aces and the deuce of clubs, and hands them to me. I put the four cards under the table, mixing them around in a face down packet, and bring them up in a little face down fan. Dave picks first, then Phil, then Antonio, leaving me with a solitary card in my hand. I turn my card face up right away; sure enough, it's the deuce of clubs, the low card. Dinner is on me again.

As accustomed as I am becoming to being the guy who never ever wins, I must admit, it's getting a little bit old at this point.

Next day, Antonio has been invited to participate in an invitation only televised poker tournament. The Game Show Network is sponsoring a "Men vs. Women" tournament, where six featured male players will play as a team against six well known women players. Upon showing up at the Union Plaza, where Antonio had put my name in at the security desk, I am surprised to find that there is no studio audience. Apparently, I'm the only name on the guest list. I'm led to a curtained-off section of the room where the taped game is going on. Inside are a trio of monitors showing the "live feed," a few technical people, an onscreen "hostess," somebody who looks like the producer of the show, and a small table where two guys are sitting riffling through a pack of playing cards.

Feeling a bit out of place, I sit down at the small table and join the two other guys. They both look up at me and offer me the briefest of acknowledgments before continuing their intense conversation. I recognize them both instantly—here I am sitting with not one, but two WSOP world champions, Greg Raymer, and Chris Moneymaker. I can't help but eavesdrop on their conversation, all the while pretending to be interested in the onscreen poker action being shown on the three monitors.

To my absolute delight, Greg and Chris are exchanging bad beat stories. Given that these are not your everyday poker guys, their bad beat stories are very different from my own common tales of miracle river cards and runner-runners. Champion level "bad beat" stories revolve around how you are no longer as lucky as you once were.

Chris laments about how, just the other day, he had all his chips in with one to come and missed a big flush draw. Greg nods his head in consolation, indicating that he understands what it means to be abandoned by the Poker Goddess. Greg tops Chris by telling the story about how, in the same week, he lost not one, but two key coin flips. Chris shakes his head solemnly. I'm tempted to interject: "What's the world coming to when a coin flip is no longer the 'sure thing' that it used to be?"

We are shortly joined by a dejected Antonio, who just got busted from his televised game. "I'm not The Guy," he tells nobody in particular. But watching him conduct his on camera "exit" interview, where he discusses how he got knocked out of the tournament, I can't help but be impressed. He really may be The Guy after all, because even though Antonio just bluffed off all of his chips on the turn, holding a straight draw, in attempt to get the top full house to toss her hand away, Antonio handled the onscreen interview with the confidence of a seasoned TV news anchor. He was polite, he spoke slowly with positive energy, never once stammering or blaming anybody but himself. This is not easy to do moments after one is knocked out of a poker tournament.

I'm always ready to leave Las Vegas after three or four days: too little sleep, too many martinis, not enough exercise, too much fun, and one too many trips to the Bellagio buffet, finally take their toll. Antonio and I will be flying back to San Francisco together. We give Dave a ride to the Las Vegas airport. Dave bemoans the fact that the six hours he will be spending en route to the East Coast will not be spent playing online poker, thus costing him several thousand dollars. In consolation, Antonio offers Dave what sounds like a "no lose" bet. Antonio proposes that he will be able to board the airplane without showing any kind of identification whatsoever. Dave is somewhat incredulous (as am I); there is no way he will be able to win that bet. Dave, ever the action-monkey, pounces on the wager. They agree on $200.

Thirty minutes later, I am sitting in my seat aboard a Southwest Airlines jet shaking my head in astonishment. Sure enough, by a combination of his persuasive charm, self-confidence, and a little deft maneuvering, Antonio actually managed to board the aircraft without showing any kind of identification. I congratulate him on pulling one over on Dave and making a quick $200.

Antonio stops shuffling his ever-present deck of Bicycles with one hand, lifts a waxed eyebrow as he flashes me a sly "Aladdin meets Bugs Bunny" smile, asking: "Seriously, Dr. Philips, would I make a bet like that if I thought I could lose? Would you bet against me?

And, as much as it pained me to admit it, I had to concede that I would not.

Rob Fulop is a video-game designer who also plays poker as a hobby. This story first appeared in Bluff *magazine.*

A Little Magic

The first time I went to the World Series of Poker, I did a lot more magic than poker playing. I remember that on the first break of the main event I walked outside to get some air with Phil Laak and we saw Huck Seed, Phil Hellmuth, and Daniel Negreanu doing the same. I did not know Huck or Daniel at the time, but somehow I ended up doing a magic trick for them. Now, this was not just any trick. It was a trick that I have only done about 15 times in my entire life because it is so difficult to pull off—let alone in front of three great poker minds trained to observe everything.

So I pulled out the deck and placed it in Huck's hand and asked him to simply name a card out loud. "Three of clubs," he said out loud. Now, we were standing about 30 feet away from the side of the Horseshoe by the Fremont Street entrance. I didn't say a word. Instead, I grabbed Huck's hand and pulled him toward the Horseshoe's entrance. As we approached the glass doors, Huck's jaw dropped to the floor as he saw the three of clubs stuck on the door—on the inside nonetheless. I'll never forget the look on all of their faces, especially Huck. Huck is one of the smartest guys I know, and he was so shocked and confused because he knew that there was not enough time for someone to have placed that card up there that fast. He thought that maybe I had all 52 cards taped all over the place and actually looked around to see if he could find any other cards. When he could not find any other cards, he came to me and said, "Antonio, you got me. I mean you really got me. I have seen a lot of card tricks, but that one really takes the cake."

That just goes to show you that even the best minds in poker can be tricked.

A couple of years later, I was back at the World Series and was becoming more known as a poker player. However, by this time, everyone knew about my magic skills. Well, they were playing the big game over at the Horseshoe. This was a cash game and not a tournament event. I was walking by, and Doyle Brunson asked if I could show them a little magic. Now, this table included Doyle, Chip Reese, Bobby Baldwin, Barry Greenstein, and Chau Giang.

I pulled out a closed deck and gave it to Bobby Baldwin and asked him to hold it. Then I took the actual deck that they were playing with, spread it out on the table, and asked Bobby to pull out a card and show it to his friends, which he did. Keep in mind that Bobby pulled the card out on his own and from the deck that they were already playing with. I then asked him to put the card back in the deck and shuffle it up. He did. I asked him if I had in any way touched the unopened deck that I had previously given him to hold. Bobby replied no. I asked him to watch closely as I took the unopened deck, pulled out the cards, and spread them across the table. As I spread the cards, only one card was faceup—the two of hearts, which as you might have guessed was in fact the card Bobby had picked. To top it off, not only was it the only card face up, it was also the only one with a blue back, while all the other cards were red backed. The guys were totally spooked.

After that, I was completely loose and proceeded to pick-pocket Chip Reese's watch, which was a big hit. Of course, I gave it back. Everyone was so nice to me, and this was before I had ever won anything. They are all just great people as well as great poker players.

At Phil Hellmuth's party, I did this spooky magic trick for Mike Sexton. This was an extremely difficult trick, so it's not one that I perform that often. But this was my first time around so many of the top poker players, and I really wanted to impress them. There were about 20 poker players around us when I asked Mike to pick out a card. Mike showed the card to everyone. Now, keep in mind that these are not casual observers. Poker players pride themselves on figuring everything out, so there were 20 sets of eyes intently studying my every movement.

I then had Mike place the card back in the deck anywhere he wanted to. I took the deck, turned it faceup, and spread it out across the table. There was one card missing. Yes, you guessed it, Mike's card was gone. Here's the kicker. I asked Mike to reach into the back pocket of his pants to see if he could feel a card in there. Mike said that there was no point in trying because it could not be there. I had to really talk Mike into reaching into his pocket. He finally did so, and I'll never forget the look on his face when he felt a card there. He pulled it out, and sure enough it was the card he had picked—the five of clubs.

I asked him if he wanted to try it again with a different card just to show that this trick would work with any card. He declined. I'll never forget how I felt when he pulled that card out of his pocket. Everyone went bonkers. It was beautiful. When you are playing poker, all eyes are on you. You can't be afraid to take chances.

I would like to give a special thanks to Layne Flack for helping me out with that trick. I could never have pulled it off without his help, and to this day he has never told a soul how I did it. And Rick Rios and Joey Burton deserve special thanks as well, because if it were not for them, I never would have made it so far in magic.

My favorite thing about doing magic is the way it makes people feel. Everyone loves magic. It brings out the kid in them. I have been so fortunate in my life to be at the right place at the right time to see someone perform magic and then have the tools to get into it. Magic is one of the most beautiful art forms on the planet, and No Limit Hold 'Em is right up there as well. I love to perform magic when I know my father is in the audience. The look on his face is priceless. He loves it more than I do, and to know that I can make him light up like that makes me very content with life.

SPEAK LIKE THE PROS

(COURTESTY OF ANTONIO AND PHIL "THE UNABOMBER" LAAK)

Liven up your poker vocabulary with these colorful expressions from Antonio and his peers.

CTB Call to bluff. Calling a bet with the intention of bluffing your opponent on a later betting round.

CTC Call to crack. When you call with some sort of garbage hand in hopes of cracking a big hand.

FBS Full-blown squeezer, which is a supertight player.

felted When a player is down to the felt, it means he has no more chips. There is nothing between him and the felt, and he is felted or broke. (Phil Laak gets full credit for coining this one.)

GFTG Good for the game. A bad player, or pigeon, who is contributing a lot of dead money is said to be good for the game.

HTS   Hurt the squeezer.

LDP   Lock-down poker. Buttoning down and playing straight and tight without trying to be too creative. Basically locking it down and going into tight poker mode. Lock down, baby!

OPTD   Open the door. When a player makes a bet he should not have and now he has opened the door for a raise that he will not be able to call.

POW   Payoff wizard. A player who calls on the river when he is beat is a payoff wizard.

SID   Squeezer in disguise. A supertight player who is projecting an image of being looser than he really is.

squeezer   Supertight player.

SST   Short-stack torture.

STW   Surfing the wa. A player who is in the zone, seeing the truth at the table and knows what is going on, is said to be surfing the wa.

How to Shuffle Your Chips Like the Pros

First, split the chips into two stacks of three. Put them side by side. Put your thumb against the left side of the left stack and put your second and third fingers against the right side of the right stack. Your index finger will now naturally sit right between the two stacks. Gently pull up on both stacks with your index finger while at the same time gently pushing in with your thumb and other fingers. That will weave the chips together, and then you can let them fall in a nice little flutter and push them together in a stack. Once you get the hand of six chips, you can work up to eight, ten, or more.

Of course, the best magic trick is to get all of your opponents' chips to move from their stacks to yours, but you already knew that, right?

Ask Antonio

(Questions Players Have Sent to My Web Site)

Dear Antonio:

Apart from the obvious stuff about math and reads and fearlessness, what do you think really separates the best tournament players from the rest of us wannabes?

Admitted Wannabe

Dear Wannabe:

You gotta love tension. It's perfectly natural for people to want to avoid tension. Top poker players thrive on tension because the only time you won't be in one is when you have busted out. And don't apologize about being a wannabe. You can't be an "is" without being a "wannabe" first.

Dear Antonio:

You are one of my favorite poker players, and I figured you were the one to ask. My question involves knowing when you are beat and when you are not. I know that when someone is betting a lot, he generally has a good hand, but when do you know when he is bluffing? When I put him on a weak hand and call what I thought was a bluff, he actually has a good hand. When I put him on a good hand, and fold, he actually is bluffing. Is there anything to look for that could help me tell if I'm beat or not? Any physical tells? Any tells in the way he bets? And is there any way to figure out when a good time to bluff is?

Thanks for your time,
Devin

Hey Devin:

That's a lot of ground to cover, so let's get to it. The most trustworthy tell is this: When they act strong they're usually weak, and when they act weak they're usually strong. That's straight from Caro's Book of Tells, *and if you haven't read it yet, definitely check it out. Also, when you're thinking about calling or folding, just ask yourself what you think the guy who's betting wants you to do, and then do the opposite. Try it. It works.*

When is it a good time to bluff? Any time you think it will work. Make sure you're bluffing against players who are smart enough to fold. Some guys, you can't get them out of the pot with a cannon, so don't waste your chips trying. One of my favorite bluffs is on a flop like 8-8-3 rainbow. No straight, no flushes, no big cards . . . how can anybody have a piece of that orphan flop? Go ahead and adopt it. Everyone else may know you're bluffing, but they still can't call.

Hey Antonio:

Being as famous as you are, women must throw themselves at you. How do you handle it?

Thank you, Alice

Dear Alice:

*You know what they say: It's a dirty job, but somebody's got to
do it.*

Dear Antonio:

They say, "There are three ways to play pocket jacks—all
wrong." What do you say about that?

Headly

Dear Headly:

*Yeah, jacks can be tricky. Trouble is, if you treat them like a big
pair and push them hard, the only hands you will get action
from are aces, kings, or queens, plus A-K, A-Q, maybe K-Q, the
kind of hands that can kill you if the board comes with even one
high card (which it always seems to do). If you treat it like a
drawing hand and just call, you're trying to flop a set, which
only happens 1 out of every 7.5 times. You could fold jacks, but
who does that?*

*Me, I just try and match the hand to the table. If my ene-
mies are weaker or looser than average, I play jacks strong. If
they're tighter or stronger than average, I play my jacks a little
more snug. And yeah, if there's a big raise, reraise, and call in
front of me, I just chuck 'em away. Jacks are good, but they're not
that good.*

Dear Antonio,

I have a question. I'm playing in a ladies' No Limit
Hold 'Em tourney at Harrah's in Lake Tahoe. I have

played and won locally here in Carson City, but never at that level. My question is this: Should I only play cards that are strong, or should I push everything and come out aggressive? Any input from you would be appreciated. Thank you.

Shady Lady

Dear Shady Lady,

First thing, don't freak out just 'cause you're playing in a "big" tournament. Those ladies pull their panty hose on one leg at a time just like you do. Second, be in it to win it. Lots of people playing in their first big-time tournament will play tighter than usual, more cautious than usual. Why? 'Cause they don't want to squander their big buy-in on an early exit. Well, you know what? That's not playing to win, that's playing not to lose, and all it'll get ya is a middle finish, way off the money.

I'm not telling you to go berserk from the first hand. You want to have good hand selection, especially while you're getting over your butterflies and figuring out who you're up against. But remember how you play when you play well: strong, confident, aggressive. That's the way to win at any level, whether on the World Poker Tour or around the kitchen table.

Dear Antonio,

I am a good poker player, and I have been playing in small tournaments in my area. I play great hands, but have been beaten by players who play small hands and end up catching straights and full houses, and my high cards don't come up on the flop when I get them and call to see the flop. I have tried to buy the pot from the beginning, but they call me with their small cards. Are the bigger tournaments like this in the beginning (before the final table)? Do people usually play smaller hands? I am frustrated with this, and it seems when I hold out for all of the good hands and play a tight game in the beginning, my chips (due to the blinds) get smaller, and the players who are playing the small hands build the big stacks. A little advice from someone I look up to would be great. Thank you for your time.

Jenna

Hey Jenna,

It sounds like you're doing everything right (though without seeing you play, I'd wonder if you're really putting enough heat on your enemies when you've got strong cards) and you're just a victim of a little thing called bad luck. Look, sister, bad players play bad cards every day, and sometimes those bad cards get there. If you let it rattle you, if you start playing that same cheese, then you're just gonna go down the drain.

In big tournaments, top players play all sorts of strange hands, but that's 'cause they know what they're doing—and more often than not they're playing the players and not really playing their cards at all. But comparing top tournaments with small buy-in events is kinda apples and oranges, ya know? Be in the game you're in. Push your big hands hard! Don't worry if they call and suck out. It won't happen forever.

If you wanna take a page from the pros, think about playing the players, not just playing your cards. When you know you're up against suck-out artists, put them on draws and then punish them when their draws don't get there. Though it seems like they hit their hands all the time (and you, never), most of the time they'll miss.

Dear Antonio,

I lack the courage of my convictions. Whether I've got a good hand or I'm driving a bluff, I have no trouble betting the flop, but I don't follow through with big bets on the turn or the river. If they don't give up on the flop, I can't help thinking they've got my number and I break off my drive. Of course this means that I get bet off pots a lot, and that can't be good for my game. How can I get guts?

Cowardly Lion

Dear Cowardly Lion,

You're right that you're making yourself a sitting duck, and you've got to get over that if you ever hope to win. Ask yourself this question: What are you afraid of? Losing money? Busting out of a tournament? These things happen every day, pal. Don't you know that losing is part of winning? Poker rewards aggression and punishes cowardice. Always has, always will. Stand the heat or split the kitchen.

If you have a question for me, I would love to hear from you. Please visit my Web site, www.magicantonio.com, for details. If you want to learn more about the World Poker Tour, please visit the WPT's Web site www.worldpokertour.com.

SUGGESTED READING

The following poker books are all great reads:

Winning Low Limit Hold 'Em, by Lee Jones. The first poker book
   I ever read. This is a good book for reinforcing the fundamentals of Limit Hold 'Em.
Super System and *Super System II,* by Doyle Brunson. The section
   on No Limit Hold 'Em by Doyle is still considered the de-
   finitive work on the subject.
Caro's Book of Poker Tells, by Mike Caro. Super book for reading
   opponents.
The Theory of Poker, by David Sklansky. Groundbreaking book
   covering general poker concepts and teaching innovative
   principles.
Machiavellian Poker Strategy, by David Apostolico. A great read to

help you adopt the right philosophy when you enter the poker room.

Ace on the River, by Barry Greenstein. A must read for anyone debating whether to be a professional poker player.

WPT: Shuffle Up and Deal, by Mike Sexton. A great entrée to poker. It reads just like Mike sounds as he hosts the World Poker Tour.

WPT: Making the Final Table, by Erick Lindgren. Erick shares his tricks of the trade on tournament poker.

Author's Note

I was born in Tehran, Iran, on December 8, 1978, where, ironically, it is illegal to possess a deck of playing cards. I moved to the United States with my family in 1988, and we settled in San Jose, California. This country is amazing. While it was hard for me to adjust and fit in at school at first, I always knew that I was going to make something of myself in the United States. I had always been interested in owning a restaurant or a bar and even considered going to culinary school.

Of course, life can be so unpredictable. Somewhere along the road to culinary school, those playing cards that would have been illegal in my home country interceded in my life in a big way. When that bartender at Left at Albuquerque asked me to pick a card, my life changed paths forever. At first, I was totally fixated with magic. I dedicated every waking minute to becoming the

Antonio with his father, Bijan, brother, Paul, and grandmother Malak.

best magician I could be. Then Scott Stewart introduced me to poker, and I put the same energy and passion into becoming the best possible poker player.

I was fortunate that my progress in poker coincided with the introduction of the World Poker Tour. I was playing the games in northern California and doing well, but I still had designs on culinary school. In fact, I was registered for classes when fate intervened. With a bankroll of only $9,000, I spent $3,000 to enter the WPT event at Lucky Chances Casino in Colma, California, during the very first year of the WPT. I ended up coming in third. Along the way, I made the televised final table, where I was shown busting poker legend Phil Hellmuth. Poker can be a funny game. I faced a critical hand with about 20 people remaining in the tournament. A player at my table raised with pocket sevens. I called with K-Q of clubs. The flop came 7-9-2 with two clubs. At that point, all of our chips went in, and my opponent had me covered. Phil Laak came over to join me, and we waited for the

Antonio at the Golden Nugget with his aunt Gigi.

turn card. The beautiful ace of clubs peeled right off the deck, and I jumped off my chair into Phil's arms. We watched to make sure that the river didn't help my opponent, and when it didn't, I was back in business. If that hand had turned out differently, I may have ended up in culinary school.

Instead, I became a professional poker player. At first, my father had a hard time understanding my new profession. Persian families are very college oriented, and mine was no different. Going to college is a prerequisite for respect, which is why my father was not thrilled with my decision to play poker. It did not take long to convince him, though. I took him to a cardroom with me and let him stand behind me as I played. I would tell him what the other players had before they turned over their cards. That was all the proof he needed that I would be all right. Now my father loves it. He often travels with me and thoroughly enjoys it. I take him to all the parties and even out clubbing once in a while. He truly is my best friend.

I would go on to a first-place finish at the L.A. Poker Classic in the second season of the WPT, winning $1.4 million dollars. That same year, I would take down my first victory and coveted bracelet at the World Series of Poker. In Iran, it is often customary for parents to set their kids up with other respectable families' children. So a Persian mother would be searching for a suitable man to take her daughter's hand in marriage. Of course, this man would have to be successful before he would be considered. Then the families would meet to discuss the idea, and, of course, the ones getting married would have to be agreeable to it. But believe me when I say that the parents have a huge influence. For the longest time, no one had ever called me or my father requesting me to meet their daughter. That all changed real fast, though. As soon as the WPT aired my win at the L.A. Classic, I must have received at least 10 phone calls from Persian mothers wanting me to meet their daughters. Funny what a little fame and fortune can do.

A professional poker lifestyle is not for everybody. The great thing about poker is that you do not have to be a pro to enjoy the game. Learn to play well, and who knows what fate has in store for you. Maybe we'll meet at the final table of the next World Poker Tour event.

ACKNOWLEDGMENTS

I would like to personally thank all the following people for their support and contribution (without their help this book would not have been possible):

Brian Balsbaugh, Phil Hellmuth Jr, Phil Laak, Annie Duke, Gabe Thaler, Rob Fulop, Glynn Beebe, Kevin O'Donnell and Elaheh Borna for all of their help and support.

Steve Lipscomb for making me a rock star and dreaming up the World Poker Tour.

Scott Stewart for introducing me to poker and making me read a poker book *(Winning Low Limit Hold 'Em* by Lee Jones).

The entire team at UltimateBet.com with a special thanks to John Vorhaus and Joanne Priam; and a very important thank you to Joey Burton and Rick Rios.

Marko Trapani and Stan Seiff for running such an awesome ship at Bay 101 (my favorite casino and original stomping grounds).

Matt Savage for believing in me since day one.

The entire gang at *Bluff* magazine.

The Shulman family with a special thanks to Allyn Shulman at *Card Player* magazine for putting me on the cover.

Everyone at the WPT with a special thanks to Shana Haitt, Andrea Green, and Melissa Feldman (my favorite).

The Brandgenuity team—especially Andy Topkins; Mathew Benjamin, Gretchen Crary, Tara Cibelli, and everyone else at HarperCollins for bringing my poker winning strategies to the written word.

A VERY special thanks to all the poker dealers, chip runners, floormen, and every single casino employee throughout the world.

David Apostolico—this man made it all possible. He is the guy behind the guy. He is my contributing writer. To say this book would not have been possible without him would be an understatement.

Doyle Brunson, Bobby Baldwin, Andrew Sasson, Tom Brightlink, and Bill Macbeth for their coolness as humans. Seeing as how these guys are the most powerful guys in Vegas and how down to earth they are makes me want to be as humble as can be.

Finally—a special thanks to all of my dear friends and family—I could not be who I am without them. I love you all.

Index

GO ALL IN WITH WORLD POKER TOUR™
WINNING STRATEGIES

WORLD POKER TOUR™:
SHUFFLE UP AND DEAL
By Mike Sexton

ISBN 0-06-076251-9 (paperback)

Shuffle Up and Deal is a solid poker primer, covering set-up, play, and basic poker strategy, along with many of the interactive elements of the WPT TV show: poker trivia, definitions of poker terms using examples from the show, profiles of WPT star players, insights into the world of professional poker, and an inside look at the show.

WORLD POKER TOUR™:
MAKING THE FINAL TABLE
By Erick Lindgren

ISBN 0-06-076306-X (paperback)

This follow-up to *WPT: Shuffle Up and Deal* provides the next level of poker strategies and insights for today's poker players. The popularity of the World Poker Tour has driven the huge spike in amateur players entering No-Limit Hold'em Tournaments. As a result the old strategies of conservative slow play are no longer effective. Only the strongest and most aggressive players like Lindgren are reaching the final tables. In this book he shares what it takes to be the last one standing. This is a must have for all poker enthusiasts.

WORLD POKER TOUR™:
IN THE MONEY
By Antonio Esfandiari

ISBN 0-06-076305-1 (paperback)

This follow-up to *WPT: Shuffle Up and Deal* from poker professional Antonio Esfandiari, with contributions from other stars of the World Poker Tour, provides strategies and insights for playing cash games. Cash games are the most commonly played version of Texas Hold'em; in fact, at this very moment, thousands are playing this non-tournament style of Hold'em in casinos, home games and online.

Learn More • Do More • Live More

⊂ Collins *An Imprint of HarperCollinsPublishers* www.harpercollins.com